A LOVELY LIFE

MELISSA MICHAELS

TEN PEAKS PRESS™
EUGENE, OR

Unless otherwise indicated, all Scripture quotations are taken from the Holy Bible, New International Version®, NIV®. Copyright © 1973, 1978, 1984, 2011 by Biblica, Inc.® Used by permission of Zondervan. All rights reserved worldwide. www.zondervan.com. The "NIV" and "New International Version" are trademarks registered in the United States Patent and Trademark Office by Biblica, Inc.®

Verses marked NRSV are taken from the New Revised Standard Version of the Bible, copyright © 1989 by the Division of Christian Education of the National Council of the Churches of Christ in the USA. Used by permission. All rights reserved.

Cover and interior design by Faceout Studio

Photos on pages 21, 22, 69, 70, 104 used by permission of Susan Heid, theconfidentmom.com. Graphics on page 222 and 223 © Tabitazn / gettyimages; Some design elements © flovie / shutterstock

Ten Peaks Press is a trademark of The Hawkins Children's LLC. Harvest House Publishers, Inc., is the exclusive licensee of the trademark Ten Peaks Press.

A LOVELY LIFE

Published by Ten Peaks Press, an imprint of Harvest House Publishers
Eugene, Oregon 97408

ISBN 978-0-7369-6321-3 (hardcover)
ISBN 978-0-7369-6322-0 (eBook)

Library of Congress Control Number: 2021947790

Printed in China

22 23 24 25 26 27 28 29 30 / RDS–FO / 10 9 8 7 6 5 4 3 2 1

As long as the earth endures, seedtime and harvest, cold and heat,
summer and winter, day and night will never cease.

GENESIS 8:22

CONTENTS

Whatever is true, whatever is noble, whatever is right, whatever is pure, whatever is lovely, whatever is admirable—if anything is excellent or praiseworthy—think about such things.

PHILIPPIANS 4:8

INTRODUCTION
Savor Every Season

Whether I'm delighting in my garden on a spring day or curling up by the fire in a well-worn chair on a winter evening, when I'm at home, all is right in my world. The days may not always be perfect, but life *feels lovely anyway.*

A lovely life is one that appeals to the heart or mind as well as to the eye.

Loveliness can grow in and around us wherever we are. Our days may not read like the pages of a fairy tale. Our homes may not be the picture-perfect ones found in our dreams. Rather, a life lived with intention *becomes* lovely, blossoming one delightful moment at a time.

The rituals and rhythms we savor for home-keeping and soul-tending are as refreshing for our states of mind as they are for our homes. They are like wearing a pair of beautifully rose-colored glasses. A rosier outlook won't just sugarcoat our homes' imperfections or make sweet lemonade from sour lemons in life; it will inspire us to frame every season with more gratitude for the beauty and grace already in front of us.

Even when (and perhaps especially when) there is a shift in seasons or in our own circumstances or the world around us, we can find our equilibrium in a familiar sense of rhythm and routine for our lives and homes.

The power of finding beauty in the humblest things makes home happy and life lovely.

LOUISA MAY ALCOTT

Our rhythms empower us to design our homes and lives in more meaningful, authentic ways. The moments we intentionally elevate will nourish our well-being, infuse more enjoyment in routine household tasks, and inspire us to celebrate the sacred wonders and gifts of every season.

Seasons will come and go, but the life we create and the rhythms we practice at home become anchors against the ebb and flow, so we can find a refuge of joy and delight in the simple pleasures of them all. In the journey ahead, we will celebrate the rhythm of each season:

SPRING OFFERS RENEWAL,

SUMMER OFFERS REFRESHMENT,

AUTUMN OFFERS RECONNECTION, AND

WINTER OFFERS REST.

We'll embrace how the seasons inspire us to make our homes lovely and tend to our souls and communities with intentional beauty.

HOME*MAKING —Creating a lovely place to live.
SOUL*TENDING —Taking care of you and those you love.

For everything there is a season.

ECCLESIASTES 3:1 NRSV

SPRING

---◆---

*See! The winter is past; the rains are over and gone.
Flowers appear on the earth; the season of singing has
come, the cooing of doves is heard in our land.*

SONG OF SOLOMON 2:11-12

RHYTHMS
FOR RENEWAL

Chirp, chirp! The birds sing their cheerful morning song outside my bedroom window. I may want to pull the covers over my head, but I admire their impulse to sing with delight! Winter has kept us cooped up too long. *Tweet, tweet!* Spring is here!

We're invited to emerge from our cozy winter nests to be a part of the beauty that's awakening. The warm sun, birdsong, and flowers are an antidote for winter blahs. I can hardly wait to open the doors, take in the intoxicating scent of lilacs, and say good morning to the first blooms. Yes, I'm *that* neighbor. The one you might see climbing up a tree in her pajamas to cut a few spring branches for a bouquet. But flowers are fleeting, and savoring these moments is what makes life lovely.

One spring, we were completing a kitchen remodel in our Seattle home. As the days passed, I became increasingly eager for the project to be finished so I could enjoy my morning coffee in peace (introvert confessions) and because I didn't want carpenters and ladders blocking the view of our magnolia tree!

Those tulip-shaped blooms and deep green leaves are a happy visual cue that this season will offer abundant gifts. The pink flowers aren't necessarily a sign that the days ahead will all be rosy, but certainly they remind me to stay rooted in hope for the renewal to come.

This season, beauty will be renewed in all the beautiful moments we can anticipate, like magnolia flowers blooming, but others will unfold in unexpected places. I'm inspired when vines find their way through cracks in concrete! No matter what this season will hold, we can be assured that beauty will bloom within and around us too.

How can you welcome beauty and renewal into your life?

MAKE SPRING LOVELY

20 LITTLE THINGS TO LOOK FORWARD TO

Find a pretty, botanical-inspired notebook, and grab your springiest pen! Start a spring dream list. Then write and respond to this: *What are 20 little things you'd like to do or experience this season?* Jot them in your notebook and get them scheduled on your calendar so you'll be prepared to have the loveliest spring.

PLAN SPRING RHYTHMS FOR RENEWAL

HOME*MAKING —Delight in renewing your surroundings.
SOUL*TENDING —Look for beauty to bloom in and around you.

GATHER LOVELY LIFE LESSONS

✦ Plant the seeds you want to bloom.

✦ Watch for lovely things around you to grow.

✦ Remind yourself to appreciate beauty in unexpected places.

HOME*MAKING
Delight in renewing your surroundings

WELCOME SPRING INTO YOUR HOME

Spring can prompt us to renew our homes and habits so that they can serve us in new ways. Start with an assessment of your needs right now. How might you bring new life into your home so you feel more inspired in it? How might your surroundings nurture your needs and hopes in this time of your life?

Make a list of spring moods and inspirational words that speak to you. These visuals can set you on a course to make small but meaningful seasonal changes.

What does home mean to you right now?

Look at your home in a fresh light. Is it an environment that will encourage you to be yourself and flourish in all the ways that you want to this season? Just as you are growing and changing as a person, your tastes and the ways your home could meet your needs will also evolve.

Begin at the front door, where the first impression and invitation to the life you want to experience will be made. With your inspirational words in mind and a sense of what you want your home to "say" to you, family, and friends when coming into your home, determine whether changes are needed. What modifications could best rejuvenate you as you walk through your door and into your home?

If you feel overwhelmed when you walk into your entry, it is a good season to simplify the space. Do a little spring refresh! Pare down the number of objects that have accumulated through the winter. Put away what isn't needed, and assign homes for items that serve you by remaining in the entryway: hooks for raincoats and umbrellas, spots for keys and dog leashes, baskets for shoes, a shelf for a plant, or whatever delights you.

The atmosphere you create through personal design and home-keeping choices will inspire you to take a deep cleansing breath as you enter your door. You should be able to exhale as you cross the threshold to your sanctuary, knowing that the stress of the world can be left outside.

SEVEN-DAY SPRING TIDY

Challenge yourself to begin the season with a seven-day spring tidy. It will help you jump-start your motivation and inspire you with immediate results!

DAY 1: Simplify your morning routine. Reorganize your makeup bag, jewelry, and accessories, and begin the day without stress so you can feel like your most beautiful self.

DAY 2: Create order in the house. Instead of scrolling through the internet, saving organizational ideas for someday, spend 30 minutes actually organizing closets or drawers! It will do wonders for your spirits.

+ Closets: Tuck away your winter wardrobe. Don't keep what you didn't wear this year! Now evaluate your spring outfits. Keep what makes you feel good and what you know you'll wear. Donate the rest. Keep a list of what items will complete your wardrobe.

+ Drawers: Fill reusable tote bags with items you run across that you don't use or need. Donate, dispose, or recycle the contents. Fill the bag again next week—delight in creating breathing room.

DAY 3: Label all the things! Cabinets, drawers, shelves, and containers are much less likely to get out of control if you designate clearly what each is for and give it a pretty label. Keep your label maker out so you can make a few a day. Everything in your house can have a home.

DAY 4: Gather your gardening supplies. Put a small shovel and cute gardening gloves in a metal farm bucket.

DAY 5: Get your cleaning tools organized. Refresh your supplies and place a nontoxic cleaner and a scrub brush under each sink with a stack of microfiber rags.

DAY 6: Lighten the layers! Fold up heavy blankets, remove winter pillow covers, roll up winter rugs, and put away wintery items.

DAY 7: Take one small step. Being overwhelmed causes procrastination. What are some other areas of your home that bring added stress? Take a small but rewarding step in the right direction.

REFRESH YOUR CLEANING ROUTINES

Freeing all the winter dust bunnies and disposing of the remainder of a dried-out holiday wreath can be rejuvenating to our spirits!

We all love the way our homes feel after a good spring cleaning, yet why are we often tempted to avoid the daily housekeeping tasks as long as possible? Maybe because they never seem to end.

To avoid a sense of dread when it comes to my daily responsibilities, I don't let myself refer to housekeeping tasks as "chores" or else I will put them off until they really do become a dreadful experience.

Instead, I want to see my home as a welcoming and beautiful refuge where I can retreat from the world, a place where the smallest of details (and yes, even cleaning!) can and should be made lovelier.

When I have a clean and shiny sink, a freshly made bed, a load of laundry folded and put away, and a tidied-up corner in my home, I feel not only more accomplished in the day but also inspired and better prepared to experience more beauty in all areas of life.

Each of my four daily housekeeping routines is what I consider a "domino decision" in the day. As a necessary task is completed or avoided, it begins tipping the experience of life further one way or another, so I begin to feel either more inspired and accomplished or more overwhelmed.

The mindset we create regarding the care and keeping of our homes becomes so integral to our success in other areas and our own well-being. I'm admittedly not a naturally tidy, organized, or type-A person, so designing a simple system for taking care of my home offers a sense of accomplishment and calm.

It's certainly not easy to romanticize doing a dozen loads of laundry, but when we put on our rose-colored glasses, we will see the blessing of having people in our lives who wear the clothes and use the towels.

My four daily routines keep me from getting distracted by my own whims or becoming stuck in my tendency to overthink and procrastinate all things. Yet even with a routine, it's important to remind ourselves that every situation won't fit neatly into our carefully structured plans for the day.

Life can still be quite lovely even with unchecked boxes on the to-do list. Above all, give grace to yourself—and to your home. Life can be a bit messy at times, but the mess is often what makes life lovely too.

Consider your own rhythm for spring housekeeping, one that speaks to you and works for you in this season of life. When will you be home to take care of it? Will you be able to care for your home on your own, or will you enlist others' support and help?

LOVE YOUR LAUNDRY

When you are intentional with home tasks, you can elevate what you are doing. You're showing love and care for yourself and your family. You're making life lovelier. Add in a few of these ideas to your routine, and you'll look at the hamper of dirty clothes in a new way.

+ Use custom scented wool dryer balls.

+ Hang special clothes or sheets with wooden clothespins on a clothesline.

+ Put your detergent in a pretty container.

+ Give your laundry space a refresh with paint, wallpaper, or artwork.

+ Hang a drying rack.

+ Upgrade your laundry bins to pretty baskets.

+ Add a plant or flowers to your laundry area.

+ Use a vintage cabinet to store your laundry supplies.

LAUNDRY
SCHEDULE
SORT *today*
WASH *later*
FOLD *maybe*
IRON *ha ha*

SPRING-CLEAN YOUR LINEN CABINET

If you've ever stared into your linen closet completely overwhelmed or found yourself tunneling through somewhat musty, old items to get to your guest set of linens, it is time to make life easier and lovelier.

+ Toss, donate, or recycle a few unloved or unused linens.

+ Replace worn towels with a fresh and fluffy new set.

+ Wipe off shelves or drawers. If you feel inspired, line them with paper!

+ If linens smell stale, toss them in the dryer with a damp washcloth or wool dryer balls scented with essential oil.

+ Use essential oil–scented cotton balls to freshen your cabinet or drawers.

+ Group like items together and stack linens neatly on the shelf so they please your eye.

+ Step back and admire your handiwork!

Yet he has not left himself without testimony: He has shown kindness by giving you rain from heaven and crops in their seasons; he provides you with plenty of food and fills your hearts with joy.

ACTS 14:17

FRESH SPRING LINEN SPRAY

Make your own spring linen spray to refresh your sheets in between washing. Give your room and/or linens a spritz before making the bed!

+ 20–40 drops pure essential oil (any combination)

+ 2 T. witch hazel

+ Combine in a 4-ounce spray bottle.

+ Add filtered water to fill the bottle.

TRY ANY OF THESE REFRESHING SPRING COMBINATIONS:

LEMON + GRAPEFRUIT + GERANIUM

LAVENDER + LEMON + EUCALYPTUS

ROSE + LAVENDER + SAGE

NORTHERN LIGHTS BLACK SPRUCE + LIME + LEMON

YLANG-YLANG + ORANGE

ORANGE + SANDALWOOD + CHAMOMILE

LAVENDER + BERGAMOT

LEMON + SAGE

LEMON + LAVENDER + ROSEMARY

TANGERINE + SPEARMINT + LEMONGRASS

BERGAMOT + LIME

CEDARWOOD + LAVENDER

EUCALYPTUS + LEMON

BERGAMOT + CEDARWOOD + GINGER

ORANGE + ROSEMARY

YLANG-YLANG + ROSE + ORANGE + CARDAMOM

LAVENDER + ORANGE + BERGAMOT + VANILLA

DO A SEASONAL SWAP, STYLE, AND SNAP

Here's a fun seasonal styling game! After you've removed the clutter from an area of your home, swap out any displayed items for items that fit the new season and style of that area. Then step back and take a photo of the space! The "after photo" makes cleaning up a rewarding challenge, but it's also interesting what you can learn from the photo you just took.

Do you love the space as it is? Does the decor feel cluttered? Unbalanced? Do the colors inspire or clash, or do the objects overwhelm you? Are the accessories too big or too small? What is missing? Don't hesitate to try again or find a photo online to inspire you. Maybe you'll prefer the look when it's pared down or freshened up with other accessories. Taking a photo can help you see the space with fresh eyes so you can make it lovelier.

Forget the former things; do not dwell on the past.
See, I am doing a new thing! Now it springs up; do you not perceive it?
I am making a way in the wilderness and streams in the wasteland.

ISAIAH 43:18-19

BRING SPRING TO YOUR NEST

After a long winter, I feel restless from staring at the same things. I think a change in scenery can be a real mood-booster.

I know for some people, a change of scenery probably means lying out on a beach somewhere. Bless. I'm all for that. But for me, a change of scenery in spring often involves a simple refresh of an area in my home.

While it's always fun to work on big projects, like a remodel or new furniture, there is so much beauty to be experienced in the little things that bring us joy. Here are five Rs to help you renew your space and your outlook.

Replace colors to create a mood. Changes in your color palette can do wonders for the mood. Don't worry if your color palette doesn't "feel like spring." What matters is how *you* feel in your home. If you need a boost of happiness or positivity in your life, punch up the vibes in your home with fresh colors.

To create a sense of peace and order, select hues that soothe you. Perhaps light neutrals and warm textures ease your stress. Maybe moody, darker tones relax your mind. If your home doesn't get a lot of natural light, some brighter or lighter shades may lift your mood. Pay attention to how you feel in your home and make adjustments!

Refresh decor for the season. Say goodbye to winter decor! Use what you have. Gather up a stack of pretty books or accessories from around the house in colors you like, display a favorite spring-inspired collection, put a bouquet in a vase, or frame a favorite family photo. Maybe hang a new piece of art, put down a cheerful rug, or repaint the walls to freshen things up!

Rearrange your shelves. Sometimes simply *moving things around a bit* will get you inspired! Dust off display shelves or a mantel and try a streamlined arrangement. Step back and admire your effort.

Reclaim treasures at flea markets. Go on a treasure hunt for a new-to-you find. Bring it home and use it to bring a different look to your space.

Renew something with spray paint. Look around your garage or closets and find a fun accessory that just needs a little spring makeover. Candlesticks, small statues, even small toy animals! Spray paint them white or a pretty spring color! It's quite inspiring what a little paint can do to refresh what we already have.

PRETTIFY YOUR PORCH
AND OUTDOOR SPACES

Now that spring is here, it's time to peek our heads out the front door to look at the *outside* of our homes again. Think about the first impressions of your home, not only for guests but also for your own family! How could you spiff up the front door and the surrounding porch area in the coming weeks to create a more welcoming curb appeal?

Start at the front door. If you still have a crunchy wreath on the door, it's a good time to say goodbye to winter so you can start fresh! Work your way around your home's outdoor spaces. Which areas could use your creative attention? When the weather cooperates, we can *spring* into action!

+ Add a welcome doormat.

+ Layer rugs for more color or pattern.

+ Add flowering plants to pots.

+ Hang a spring flower basket.

+ Install a new door knocker and light fixtures.

+ Update your address plate.

+ Add accessories: chairs, an umbrella stand, birdhouses, wind chimes, or lanterns.

+ Paint the front door a fun spring color.

+ Refresh the front steps and walkways with a new coat of deck paint or concrete stain.

+ Paint old furniture and accessories for the porch.

+ Hang window boxes or shutters.

+ Add a pea gravel walkway or patio.

+ Revive an old shed and create a she-shed, potting shed, or retreat.

APRIL SHOWERS BRING MAY FLOWERS

Even if the rain continues to pitter-patter on the roof or life is raining on your parade, slip on your cheery yellow rain boots to make the best of it. Remember, April showers will bring May flowers.

You can be growing, thriving, and creating during this season…don't let the elements or other people's expectations put a damper on your life!

Grab your cutting shears and head outside. Putter around the yard, grab sprigs of greenery, wildflowers, or even a few pretty weeds to line up in vases on the kitchen windowsill. They will bring a dose of joy and sunshine to your day.

If you don't have an outdoor garden or blooming flowers yet, treat yourself to a grocery store bouquet. If you buy a large one, you can even divide the flowers among smaller bud vases to spread the feeling of spring throughout your home. I also like to buy small plants at our local garden store. They last far longer than a bouquet and bring just as much happiness to my home.

If you have a garden and a library, you have everything you need.

TULLIUS CICERO

SOUL*TENDING

*Look for beauty to bloom
in and around you*

PUT A NEW SPRING IN YOUR STEP

It's easy to get into a rut in our lives, doing the same things day in and day out. We go through the motions but miss out on the sense of joy and wonder we used to feel. We sit at the same table, eat the same foods, follow the same routines. Maybe we go on the same vacation. We listen to the same music. We mindlessly reach for our phones to scroll through the same ideas and inspirational images day after day.

There's certainly nothing wrong with routines, but when life starts to feel stale or stagnant, the change in seasons can inspire us to renew habits—and renew the atmosphere in our homes too. If you're open to trying something new, life will feel more inspiring again.

+ Eat breakfast outside to watch the sunrise.

+ Drink your coffee out of a different cup.

+ Switch the lamps in your bedroom for the ones in the living room.

+ Plant a new-to-you type of flower in the pots on your porch.

+ Hang airy spring curtains in place of winter ones, just for fun.

Make this a season of renewal and rejuvenation in many areas of your life. A change in the routine just might be the spring transformation your home, heart, and soul crave the most.

SAVOR SPRING SENSES

Fresh air and flowers are such a welcome gift after a season of hibernation inside. Get outside, dig in the garden, and soak in the scents of nature.

Take a spring walk around your yard or neighborhood. Look at the shapes of budding leaves. Take note of what unexpected combinations of colors and textures move you. Pay attention to the unique sounds in springtime. Watch how nature unfolds its beauty as the days and weeks go by! Observe the layers of loveliness. Take time to close your eyes and breathe more deeply.

Throw open the windows! Let more sun into your rooms to light the dark corners. Use each of your senses to enhance the mood in your home. You'll discover which senses speak the most intimately to your emotions, your heart, and your soul in this season. How could seeking these gifts more regularly become a part of your spring rhythm?

When I feel overwhelmed or have trouble relaxing or concentrating on anything meaningful, I find it so helpful to pause and take note of any distracting sounds in the background of my surroundings.

Perhaps I'm a highly sensitive person, but jarring or unnerving sounds around me are a distraction. Dogs barking in my ears or the sounds of other people or electronics filling the air around me make it difficult for my mind to escape.

Nature's soundtrack is the absolute best for relaxing my body and mind. Taking time for a trip to a sandy beach where I can hear the ocean waves, or stopping for a rest by a babbling brook—these things do wonders to soothe my soul.

To refocus my attention when I'm indoors, I often put on my noise-blocking headphones and play nature sounds. It's incredible what a bird chirping in a tree or gentle waves rolling against the shore can do to transport my mind to a more inspired and restful place.

What are the spring sounds that inspire you? Set up your spring playlist.

Let your springtime observations inspire you. They can help you to develop a more innate awareness of the power the senses have on your mood. Think about how well you respond to these changes in the season.

The more you observe and discover what fills, soothes, and energizes you, the more you'll subconsciously and intentionally begin to infuse what you need for your own well-being into your life and home.

KEEP YOUR EYES ON THINGS ABOVE

I love to take walks. One spring day as I strolled through the neighborhood, I happened to look up and see two gorgeous bald eagles soar effortlessly above me, their majestic wings propelling them across the vibrant blue spring sky. They eventually circled in for a smooth landing, each selecting their own branches on which they wanted to rest. Soon they began carrying on a lively conversation, squawking back and forth at each other in their secret eagle language. Moments later, a hawk joined in the birds' chatter, sharing a few choice opinions of his own from his perch on the pine tree across from them.

It was truly a miracle to be able to watch such beautiful creatures and hear them as they were communicating with each other in their habitat up in the trees!

Thank goodness I wasn't looking down at my phone at that moment! I would have missed the miraculous scene right above me. When we start to look up rather than down, we see beauty around us through the lens of the soul. We'll sense more wonder in spring, the fluffy clouds, the birds, the stunning sunsets, the petals of a flower, the kindness of our neighbors, and the faces of people we love.

This week, jot down the times that you catch yourself needlessly scrolling your phone out of habit or being distracted from the present. Take more time to be in the moment, to see and feel the world around you and how it speaks to your soul.

◇

Set your minds on things above, not on earthly things.

COLOSSIANS 3:2

SIX BENEFITS OF A STROLL

There are many reasons to move more. Working out and attending exercise classes or running groups may be what flashes before us on social media or advertisements, but there is much value in simple movement that refreshes body and spirit. Savor a stroll and see which of these benefits is your favorite:

+ uplifts your mood

+ feeds your spirit through a connection with nature

+ delivers a natural vitamin D treatment

+ creates space to let your mind wander

+ gets you away from technology

+ moves your body toward health and energy

The Lord is my shepherd, I lack nothing. He makes me lie down in green pastures, he leads me beside quiet waters, he refreshes my soul. He guides me along the right paths for his name's sake. Even though I walk through the darkest valley, I will fear no evil, for you are with me; your rod and your staff, they comfort me. You prepare a table before me in the presence of my enemies. You anoint my head with oil; my cup overflows. Surely your goodness and love will follow me all the days of my life, and I will dwell in the house of the Lord forever.

PSALM 23

EXPERIENCES TO EMBRACE

There is so much to enjoy about this season. Don't miss out. I hope this starter list helps you create your own ongoing roster of ways you want to appreciate spring.

+ Watch the sunsets.

+ Go to drive-in movies.

+ Stargaze at nighttime.

+ Study the petals of flowers and plants.

+ Watch the butterflies and bees.

+ Learn birdsong.

+ Enjoy concerts in a park.

+ Visit the zoo and learn facts about the animals.

+ Learn to make a new seasonal dish.

+ Visit a local forest, lake, or stream.

+ Make your own signature perfume with floral scents.

+ Keep a notebook of spring moments savored.

+ Visit a local flower farm and select a few favorites for your own garden.

+ Go on a walk to notice and savor spring.

Isn't it splendid to think of all of the things there are to find out about? It just makes me feel glad to be alive, it's such an interesting world.

LUCY MAUD MONTGOMERY, *ANNE OF GREEN GABLES*

NURTURE YOUR WELL-BEING OUTDOORS

Quite possibly the most anticipated part of this new season for me is spending time puttering around my backyard tending to flowers and plants. Caring for plants is a pleasure in any season, but in the spring, the fun is doubled as I can enjoy plants inside and out.

You may or may not have a green thumb, and you may not even have an outdoor space, but finding ways to benefit from the healing power of plants will refresh you in unexpected ways. Plants nurture our well-being as we tend to them. You will look forward to the times you spend in nature and experience a sacred and healing connection to the earth.

Even if you have very little space to work with, you can design a perfect destination to enjoy all spring and summer. Combine elements of beauty and comfort into an outdoor room. With a dedicated spot, privacy, and shade, you'll have a welcoming place to retreat to.

Treat your porches, patios, and garden spaces as an extension of your home. Each area should have a specific purpose and an inviting style.

What is an outdoor mood that would inspire you? Your garden should nurture you. Do you want it to feel peaceful or energized? Simple or elaborate? Fun or restful? Modern or old world?

Include inspiration from a charming restaurant or the mood of a memorable trip as you design a dining spot. Create a miniversion of your favorite outdoor space in your backyard.

What are some activities that you'd like to incorporate? Start with a list of things you would enjoy doing.

Do you enjoy gardening? Reading? Playing games? Eating dinner outside? Hosting friends and family? Playing with the dogs? Taking naps?

Create outdoor rooms that serve your family. Ensure they will be comfortable enough to spend time in and feel welcoming to those who will use them. Think about the time of day each might be used and design them with elements to make the most of the weather too—umbrellas or trees for shade, sun for gardening, and so on.

Indoor and outdoor spaces can be designed similarly. Outside you can use fences and exterior walls and trees and plants to help create a sense of privacy and "walls" for your outdoor rooms.

Even if you don't have trees nearby, you can create a space on a deck or patio with small patio-sized trees placed in pots. The impact of potted plants and trees can be quite dramatic! To create more dimension and height, I often use a taller pot or set plants on small tables or benches. You can also add a garden trellis to a pot on a deck to create more privacy in an exposed space.

Create a Pretty Potting Area

Set up a charming spot to keep gardening shovels, trowels, seeds, watering cans, pots, gloves, soil, and fertilizer. You can use anything as a potting table; try a vintage cart, old dresser, or table.

A destination like this is versatile. It will not only inspire you to connect with nature in creative ways but could also be used as a summer drink station or an entertaining station with silverware, glasses, and napkins.

PRETTY PLANT LABELS

Nurture yourself and those you love with spring's organic beauty! Potted herbs in a kitchen garden or set on a sun-drenched table will add charm to a room, flavor to your meals, and spring fragrance to the air.

Buy your herbs and place them in spring containers. Then make your own markers for a creative touch. They are easy, adorable, and fun to do. You can make them yourself, involve the family, or gather a group of friends for a spring crafting night. Here are the materials you'll need:

+ small wooden stakes

+ painter's tape

+ paint

+ label maker or permanent marker

Tape off the ends of small wooden stakes and paint them with off-white paint on one side and a color of your choosing on the tip. Label them with the herb names using a label maker or handwrite them with a permanent marker.

By the way, a small tray of potted herbs with these personalized markers also makes a great hostess gift for any spring events or garden parties you attend.

WELCOME FRIENDS IN

As our friends and neighbors eagerly leave their wintery nests looking for sunshine and signs of life, spring is a natural season to want to meet up with old friends and build new relationships.

We all need to feel like we belong. I'll admit, though, as an introverted homebody, I sometimes need the nudge to get outside in the springtime and connect with humans again (and to seek a community in real life, not just enjoy the friends living in my computer).

+ *Initiate hospitality.* Offer a genuine, heartfelt invitation to friends or neighbors with a date on the calendar (not just a "we should get together sometime!"). An in-person invite is lovely, of course, but a casual text or personal message will do.

+ *Set up a get-together on a short time line.* A short time line offers the added motivation to open the doors to friendship before the season is over (and bonus, it's an opportunity to do just enough spring cleaning that you'll be inspired by your efforts too).

+ *Keep gatherings simple and fun.* Meaningful connections can thrive in a comfortable setting. An elaborate meal or a house that is clean from top to bottom isn't required. People crave authentic relationships, not perfect lives they can't relate to.

+ *Be a blessing.* Set an atmosphere for connection, prepare a meal to nourish, and create moments where lifetime memories will be made.

Spring brings an elevated mood to the neighborhood, so it's a lovely season to bring friends and family together around the table, making it an extra special experience for everyone (including you!)! Casually themed gatherings can grow friendships through relaxed but joyful experiences with others.

REASONS TO GATHER IN SPRING

When the sun pours into my home, I am more eager to let people come into my home. I emerge from the hibernation mood of winter. Open the drapes so you can see the beauty springing forth outdoors and open your home to share in the renewal of relationships. Here are a few reasons to gather or themes for your get-togethers this spring:

+ honor a mom

+ celebrate a dad

+ indoor garden party

+ Easter (egg hunt!)

+ springtime outdoor tea party

+ girls' night in

+ graduation celebrations

+ bridal and baby showers

+ housewarming or welcoming new neighbors

+ end of the school year

SET A SPRINGTIME TABLE

Gather an assortment of seasonal branches, greenery, and flowers for a center-piece. For an unexpected twist, arrange them in a unique vessel (try a metal or ceramic planter, a pottery crock, or a vase placed within a sturdy woven basket).

+ *Make a visual feast!* Use what you have on hand to create a lovely display. Small cake stands or pedestals, baskets, carafes, or pretty trays can highlight, corral, or elevate whatever you place on them.

+ *Use light and airy linens.* Bring a charming and relaxed spring atmosphere to your gathering with crisp linens. Or try using a roll of pretty spring wrapping paper down the center of your table as a creative runner!

+ *Round up the white plates.* Create a simple and stunning table with white plates. They complement every occasion and season. Pair them with colorful or patterned bowls or salad plates for a more eye-catching look, or add texture by layering plates on top of woven chargers.

+ *Create a delightful spring beverage table.* Set up a buffet table, a nearby console or sofa table, or even an entry cabinet to serve coffee, tea, lemonade, or sparkling water as your guests come in. What you serve doesn't have to be fancy to make people feel special.

PERSONALIZE A SPRING CENTERPIECE

+ Start with a pretty bowl, tray, or basket.

+ Add organic elements. Mix it up with real and faux fruit and flowers.

+ Don't worry about arranging it perfectly; just get creative and have fun!

Creative Vessels

GALVANIZED POTS	WOODEN CRATES	SUGAR BOWLS AND CREAMERS
PAINTED TIN BUCKETS	VINTAGE COLANDER	FAUX NEST
ANTIQUE TINS	PATTERNED BOWLS	CHILDREN'S RAIN BOOTS
GLASS BOTTLES OR JARS	PICKLE CROCKS	LANTERNS
VINTAGE POTS	WOVEN BASKETS	TERRARIUMS
PRETTY TEA KETTLES	PITCHERS	PATTERNED FLOUR AND SUGAR CROCKS
	TIERED TRAYS	
	CAKE PLATES	

Inspiring Elements

TULIPS	AIR PLANTS	FAUX EGGS AND BIRDS
DAISIES	FERNS	TWIGS
WILDFLOWERS	EUCALYPTUS	SMALL PLANTS
CHERRY BLOSSOM BRANCHES	CABBAGE	PRETTY ROCKS
ORCHIDS	LIMES	LINEN
MOSS	LEMONS	SPRING FABRICS
SUCCULENTS	ORANGES	PAPER FLOWERS OR PRETTY STICKERS

MIX-AND-MATCH SALAD

Mix salad greens, something with a little crunch, something sweet, and something salty. Mix and match these yummy options, and then munch on the easiest, most personalized salad you've ever had.

SPRING LETTUCE MIX	OLIVES
THINLY SLICED RADISHES	CHERRY TOMATOES
AVOCADO	WALNUTS
MANDARIN ORANGES	APPLES
SLICED CUCUMBERS	CARROTS
SLICED ALMONDS	DATES
SUNFLOWER SEEDS	GOAT CHEESE, FETA, OR A VEGAN ALTERNATIVE
HEMP SEEDS	QUINOA
CRACKED PEPPER	LENTILS
BEETS	

Top with a lemon vinaigrette made of extra virgin olive oil, a squeeze of fresh lemon, balsamic vinegar, or salt and pepper.

SPRING LOVE LETTERS

+ Put a pot of spring flowers on a friend's porch.

+ Donate to a worthy cause.

+ Smile at strangers when you're on a walk.

+ Drop off a fresh garden salad to a friend.

+ Invite neighbors to roast marshmallows around the firepit.

◇

A single act of kindness throws out roots in all directions,
and the roots spring up and make new trees.

AMELIA EARHART

SUMMER

——◇——

*I believe the nicest and sweetest days are not those on which
anything very splendid or wonderful or exciting happens,
but just those that bring simple little pleasures, following
one another softly, like pearls slipping off a string.*

L.M. MONTGOMERY

RHYTHMS FOR REFRESHMENT

The first day of summer always felt magical as a kid. I remember waking up in the morning without a care in the world, playing barefoot on the lawn from dawn until dusk, and riding a bright-green bicycle, popsicle in one hand and two ponytails flying through the air. Life felt simpler, running through sprinklers in a bathing suit and bright-pink goggles, not worried for a minute how I looked or spent my time. I was just living my best life, delighting in the simple pleasures and refreshments of the season.

Of course, life is understandably more complicated and less carefree as adults. But what if we live more freely and lightly this summer, letting ourselves play more and enjoy our days?

Instead of staying stuck inside on the treadmill of busyness, what if we step outside to feel the sunshine on our shoulders and twinkling sand between our toes? Maybe we should stop working harder to spend more on a dream vacation, and instead slow down to embrace a dream life, a good book, and a refreshing morning on the porch. Perhaps watching the birds, strolling through a park, or having a free evening to splash with the kids in the kiddie pool is just what we need to feel more alive and more fully ourselves.

Everyone could benefit from more laughter, carefree adventures, and light-hearted moments of fun. If you were to design this season like a memorable childhood summer, what are the memories you'd want to make? Stitch these lighter, more carefree moments together in your heart so the memories become like a well-loved quilt, ready to embrace you with a sense of happiness, warmth, and comfort when you need them the most.

MAKE SUMMER LOVELY

───────◇───────

20 LITTLE THINGS TO LOOK FORWARD TO

Start a summer notebook. Create your list of things you love about this season. Then write and respond to this: *What are 20 little things you'd like to do or experience this summer?* Once your priorities and dreams are listed in your notebook, get them scheduled on your calendar. Create margins in your week for play and memory-making, and you'll feel carefree!

PLAN SUMMER RHYTHMS FOR REFRESHMENT

HOME*MAKING —Create a fresh and pretty atmosphere.
SOUL*TENDING —Find joy and refreshment in the carefree moments.

GATHER LOVELY LIFE LESSONS

+ Make a summer bucket list that will refresh you.

+ Find joy in the simple pleasures.

+ Make room for the carefree life you always dream about.

HOME*MAKING
Create a *fresh and pretty atmosphere*

PLAN A SUMMER STAYCATION

I'm a homebody through and through, but I still need to get away from it all now and then. A quaint hotel somewhere in a charming seaside town will forever be my destination of choice. Retreating to a room piled high with fluffy pillows, a stack of mystery books on the nightstand, and coastal air blowing through the balcony door? Winter, spring, summer, or fall, give me the key to the room and I'm there.

If we don't fully love living in our own homes, we probably feel the need to escape more often than we'd like to admit. Our homes should welcome us with open arms and inspire us to live a life we love all year.

What is your ideal vacation destination?

Why does it inspire you?

How does being there make you feel?

How could you bring a get-away-from-it-all mood to your home?

Bringing elements and the mood of a vacation destination to your own home will nurture your well-being in similar ways.

Desiring a relaxing "get away from it all" mood motivates me to take better care of my home to serve our family in the way I want it to. I try to treat my home as if it's my favorite destination. That perspective spurs me on throughout the season to find little ways I can refresh my surroundings and things that I can do to make me feel (and remind me to be) more relaxed, happy, and full of joy—like I'm on vacation every day.

Whether it's a practical or seasonal element such as a basket of sandy flip-flops placed by the door, or imperfections like the dings and scratches on hardwood floors (at our house, they're from dogs who screech around corners to greet us when we return!), it's what we choose to see and feel when we are at home that can remind us to be grateful for the life we live and love.

REFRESH THE MOOD OF YOUR HOME

One summer, my family and I were invited to spend a few days in a gorgeous home on the Washington coast. My friend Susan and her husband had custom-designed a dream house to be their full-time residence in a darling coastal community.

Their house was charming inside and out, had plenty of room for the whole family to relax, a cozy fireplace for stormy nights, a spectacular view of the ocean, and more. It had everything I could ever dream of in a vacation home! What a treat to spend time there!

For years when our kids were young, my parents owned a beautiful family beach house on the Oregon coast, where our family spent many weekends and holidays. It was perfect, with sandy floors from walks on the beach, books for reading and games for playing, window seats for napping, and bunk beds filled with late-night laughter from siblings and cousins.

When that house was sold, we had to get more creative with our vacation destinations going forward, but it inspired me to create our own staycations at home. We miss the beach house so much, but we never forget how it felt to be there. We will always carry the memories and bring the feelings of our summer home with us, wherever we go.

FIVE WAYS TO DESIGN A CAREFREE ATMOSPHERE

We can make our homes inviting and carefree in simple ways. It doesn't have to be a dream house or filled with the latest decor to bless the people inside with abundance. No matter how big or humble our houses might be, they are shelters to be grateful for.

We don't need the ideal setting, furniture, or architecture; it's about the mood and memories we create within our own four walls. Summer is a season to relax and allow imperfection and beauty to come together in authentic ways as we create our own favorite destinations.

1. *Set up a relaxing destination.* The lazy days of summer call for relaxation. When you head to a tropical vacation, next to spending time at the pool or on the sandy beach, you are probably also looking forward to that cool, quiet corner of the hotel where you can lounge with your fruity drink, read a book, or fall asleep. Set up a spot in your home to do the same! A window seat with an abundance of soft pillows or a lounge chair on the deck can be an inviting destination to read those summer books you want to indulge in.

2. *Bring in a summer mood.* As soon as June rolls around each year, I'm all about feeling the summer beach house vibes. Remove any heavy drapes, throw blankets, and bedding. Roll up heavy rugs and clear surfaces of clutter for a lighter, airier-feeling home. Bring in some throw pillows and cotton rugs in summer hues and patterns to transform your winter house into a summer vacation cottage.

3. *Make things pretty.* It's the little things that help me set a mood for a life I love living. Every summer, I put a vase on the dining room table. It's such a seemingly insignificant thing, but it becomes a pretty, visual reminder to keep the table clutter-free. With a clear surface and a vase on the table, I'm more inspired to savor simple pleasures like seasonal foliage in my home. Whether I run out to the backyard to cut a fresh bouquet or treat myself to one from a local farmer's market, I enjoy my summer so much more when there are fresh flowers on my table each week.

4. *Collect and display staycation art.* My husband and I have always collected line drawings, small paintings, and watercolors from our vacations. It's fun to do the same with "staycations." Look for artsy postcards, notecards, or even menus around your hometown when you visit fun coffee shops, restaurants, boutiques, parks, or other local destinations. Frame the memories in a gallery wall to help you remember those special times and destinations.

5. *Make backyard memories.* Some of the best summer memories can be made right in your own backyard. Divide your backyard into activity zones to make it an even more desirable destination! What part of your yard will you go to eat? To play? To unwind? To garden?

Clean off the lounge chairs and blow up the kiddie pool. Set up an outdoor movie screen. Gather supplies for s'mores, and you've got yourself the best kind of summer vacation, complete without traffic or stress to get there!

ORANGE + BERGAMOT SUGAR FOOT SCRUB

Use that relaxing destination you set up in your home while boosting your mood with citrus-infused pampering. Make a foot scrub to pamper yourself for summer while indulging your senses! Create lovely things that will make you feel more lovely too.

+ 2 cups granulated sugar

+ ¼ cup almond or coconut oil

+ 4 drops orange essential oil

+ 4 drops bergamot essential oil

Optional:

+ Dried lavender and rose petals

+ 2–3 drops vitamin E oil

Combine the sugar, coconut oil, and essential oils in a glass bowl. Add the dried flowers and vitamin E oil if desired. Mix thoroughly. Massage the scrub into your feet for five minutes. Rinse with warm water and pat dry! Store in a glass jar with an air-tight lid.

DECLUTTER + DUST = RELAXING SPACES

A summer house is designed to soak in the beauty of fresh, pretty, and clean spaces. Bring that mood to your home with an easy declutter and dust session.

Look at your floors, counters, and horizontal surfaces. These surfaces become gathering places for seasonal mementos alongside odds-and-ends brought out to serve us in busy moments. Understandably so, they provide a convenient place to set things down so you can get on with the business and enjoyment of life. But if we default to this, our surfaces display things that no longer serve or inspire us. Ask yourself these questions:

Is what you are keeping on display meaningful, pretty, or necessary?
Are the items sitting where they belong?
Do they add or distract from the mood you want in your home?

Choose a surface for a ten-minute declutter and dust. Go through items and decide whether they inspire and serve you right now or if they should be moved elsewhere. Place what needs to be kept in its intended home (such as a drawer, file folder, hutch, or shelf). Don't overthink it! Trust that first response. You will feel so much better. And I guarantee you, you will want to do it again.

Once the surface is cleared, dust it, and don't put the clutter back! If it's a spot that tends to be a clutter magnet (these are usually found in main areas of the home), declare it a clutter-free zone all summer long.

When you spot a wayward item later in the week, take it to its home right away.

If you want to give the surface some style, add a bowl of summer shells or a summery striped throw rug on the floor. Pretty accessories can inspire you to keep the area clean and clutter-free.

When you...
make room for what is lovely
make room for the life you want to live
make room for grace in the process

You...
honor your space and how you feel in it
let go of what no longer serves you
bring in only what speaks life to you

CREATE LOVELY "GET READY SPACES"

You're lovely! Make your spaces lovely too so they inspire you and reflect who you are.

Pretty up the closet. Set up a pretty clothes closet where your summer attire will be organized and can be enjoyed. Start by paring down. Select only items that fit your body. Go through your clothes and pull together your signature outfits. Casual striped T-shirts, flowy floral dresses, and cute new tennis shoes are always at the top of my summer wardrobe list. What's on your list? Make room for your current style in your closet!

Beautify the bathroom. Create a bathroom that reflects your sense of beauty by simplifying. Don't keep old skincare products or makeup. Sort through your beauty products and toss anything that you don't use or that invites toxins into your routine or home. Invest in less stuff and stick to quality, toxin-free products that enhance your beauty! Less junk in the bathroom means your surroundings will be more lovely too.

One thing I ask from the LORD, this only do I seek: that I may dwell in the house of the LORD all the days of my life.

PSALM 27:4

SUMMERIZE YOUR DECOR

A less-is-more approach can offer a fresh look to your home this summer, but you can still add a touch of personal flair with your favorite mix of summer texture, color, or pattern.

One of my favorite summer-style swaps is to add fun tea towels in my kitchen. Striped, floral, coastal, or preppy plaid, what is your summer tea towel style? Drape your favorite across the sink as your reward after you polish it. Or hang a few pretty towels on hooks for a summer-style statement, like a little work of art! Let your family know which towels are decorative (make it clear these are meant to stay pretty—that is, you do not want them to be used to clean their dirty shoes).

It was you who set all the boundaries of the earth;
you made both summer and winter.

PSALM 74:17

Here are more ways to welcome summer into your home:

+ Introduce lively layers or fun patterns (like striped rugs, floral pillows, a quilt, or a patterned lampshade).

+ Mix, match, and have fun with a new look.

+ Stack books in sets of lively colors.

+ Put plants in light-toned woven baskets or ceramic pots!

+ Paper a wall with fun removable wallpaper or paint it with a stencil.

+ Remove heavy curtain panels or replace them with something light and airy.

+ Swap out cozier pillow covers for a lighter fabric or summer hue.

+ Hang botanical artwork.

+ Switch out your kitchen towels for a fresh, clean set.

+ Display a collection of recycled or vintage glass bottles or jars in shades of blue and green.

+ Add a seasonal doormat to your porch.

+ Layer rugs to add summer texture, patterns, or more color.

+ Set up an outdoor seating area.

+ Cover a tired table or bench with a Turkish towel or picnic blanket.

+ Touch up your home furnishings with fresh paint (like a fireplace, cabinets, doors, frames, tables, walls, and so on).

+ Create an inspiration board for a summer room or project. Gather magazine photos to make old-school scrapbooks or make an online mood board.

+ Play musical chairs, experiment with less furniture, or put accessories in new rooms.

INSPIRE YOUR COLOR PALETTE

Even if you are a neutral-loving girl, infusing a bit of color in various ways throughout your home can bring a new spark of happiness to a summer space.

You don't have to change your entire color scheme to summerize your home's palette, although a new coat of paint on the wall is always an option!

What colors do you love? Look online for inspirational rooms and accessories in hues that speak to you right now. Take a walk outside and observe the seasonal colors around you. Look for a pretty color in an inspirational piece, perhaps a rug, pillow, or piece of artwork. What drab colors could you remove from your current palette?

Play up a new color by using it in several places around the room. Maybe a sea green, a deep gold, a navy blue, or vibrant citrus-inspired hues like lemon or coral.

There are so many simple ways to refresh your color palette. I like to collect colorful dessert plates and napkins for our table because they are simple to switch for the season or on a special occasion. Colorful dishes and table linens bring so much delight when you see them as you open a cabinet or drawer or set the table for the evening meal.

If you're really feeling brave, hang your colorful plates on the wall! They don't have to be permanent, but once you see them there, you just might decide they should be!

It's also simple to create a new seasonal palette with a quick switch of accessories—swap artwork to incorporate brighter colors or depict a summer scene.

SOUL*TENDING
Find joy and refreshment in the carefree moments

SIMPLIFY YOUR SUMMER RHYTHM

Summer is a season when our home and family rhythms shift to accommodate children being home from school, time off from work, or other adjustments to our daily routines. We might be making summer memories with our kids, shuffling them to the pool, or shuttling them to summer camp, but it's important to find a rhythm for this season that also recognizes our own needs. We all know we can't pour from an empty cup! We need to refresh ourselves too.

Creating a simple summer rhythm doesn't stifle the freedom we long for in summer. It allows us to carve out more freedom for what we want from the season. Intentionality inspires us to use our days to *become* who we want to be and feel what we want to feel, not just to do what needs to be done at the moment. A comfortable rhythm for our days keeps us mindful of our time and present needs. It inspires us to make choices that sustain our health and well-being.

If you have kids, you may have already made a list of summer activities for them. What activities are important to you? What do you anticipate will drain your physical energy, uplift your emotional wellness, or fill your spiritual cup in this season?

Make a list of your personal summer priorities. How can you fit them into your days, weeks, and months? Keep your expectations fluid enough so that summer feels carefree yet tethered to the anchors you've established for your well-being.

Without the delicate balance of a sustainable rhythm in our day-to-day lives, little things pile up to become big things that overwhelm us. Understanding the need to set priorities and establish habits that honor all of who we are helps clarify our daily decisions.

A moment of dedicated quiet time before a day of "extroverting" can fill the cup of an introvert. A vacation from a dreaded routine can refresh us in between busy seasons. Summer presents us with an opportunity to break free from unhealthy ruts we've found ourselves in to find a healthier ebb and flow of life that will restore us.

A new season is a call to reassess our activities, revisit priorities, and make adjustments that can bring our states of well-being into better balance. It's not always easy to find it, but a rhythm can help us slow the pace of productivity and find health, healing, and restoration.

Make room for quiet contemplation and time for beauty-seeking and carefree days—with times of rest, times of energy, times of solitude, and times of connection. The right rhythm in this season will be like breathing; it's necessary for life. When one part of your home, body, mind, or soul is neglected, it begins to unravel the delicate balance of the whole. Learn to incorporate each aspect of your well-being into your daily life and adjust until the rhythm feels right.

SET SUMMER INTENTIONS

A restorative and memorable summer feels infinitely more possible for us and our family when we start it out with the right intentions. Begin the season with reasonable aspirations. Include freedom, responsibility, and grace for all who live in your home. Creating the right tone in your home will reap great rewards, because when you feel your best, life is lovelier for you, and you have more to give to those you love.

Freedom to slow down.

Freedom to let go of the unnecessary.

Freedom for everyone to enjoy the things they want to experience in the summer.

Responsibility for everyone to pitch in with housework to make summer better for all.

Responsibility to set healthy boundaries but relax unnecessary rules.

Grace to let go of unrealistic expectations.

Grace to be imperfect, in progress, and in the moment!

Set a pace for summer that will reflect your family's priorities and goals but will also fill your body, mind, and soul with what you need.

PREPARE FOR FUN-FILLED SUMMERS

Have a plan of action for summer so your family stays active and connected. There is so much joy to be had during this season of long, sunny days.

1. Plan ahead for activities you will need to sign up for (many camps and classes fill up by winter and spring, so schedule as early as possible).

2. Set up the grill and backyard barbecue area so you will be ready for spontaneous fun.

3. Prepare a garden so everyone can participate and get the most joy out of it all summer!

4. Make a list of summer games, craft ideas, and hobbies you or your family would enjoy. Gather the supplies and keep them on hand for fun family nights or for the "Mom, I'm bored" days.

5. Suggest a summer reading plan. Have every family member make a list of their top five summer books and then head to the library or bookstore, or get them on your electronic reading device. Check in with one another during the season to discuss the books or to share highlights from the reading adventure.

SOOTHE YOUR SOUL WITH
BACKYARD DESTINATIONS

When we first moved into our home, the unlevel and cracked concrete on the small patio outside our kitchen made it a downright frightening and dangerous area. With a fresh new surface, potted plants, and furniture, it has been completely transformed into an inviting oasis. In a potting area on each corner of the patio, we planted climbing white roses and star jasmine, so the scent is heavenly!

I long to live in a small cottage in Nantucket. I haven't been there in person (yet!), but I know between the charm of the shingled homes and the sea air, it would feel like home to me. One summer, I brought my own version of Nantucket home to our patio. We put four white Adirondack chairs around a small, round, portable firepit. Blue-and-white-striped cushions on the chairs made them more comfortable and gave them a charming, nautical look. It became the perfect summer spot to sit and enjoy morning coffee.

We put a coffee table and a weather-resistant sofa on an outdoor rug and added a complete dining table with chairs nearby to have room for the whole family. This outdoor room doubles the living space of our home.

You can refresh old outdoor furnishings with a new coat of exterior paint and give them more comfort and style with updated cushions that are easy to clean and resistant to rain. We keep our patio furniture and cushions outside from spring through fall and only bring them under cover if it's going to rain for more than a day. They've lasted for years in our climate. Once winter arrives, we put the cushions in our outdoor storage shed, but we leave the furniture out due to lack of storage.

Create charming outdoor spaces where you can retreat to and friends can gather and dine. Hang a hammock near a small bubbling fountain for the ultimate backyard oasis. Who needs a spa? You can make your own water feature with a large pot and a portable fountain motor!

Even if you don't have much room to work with, one comfortable spot to sit and read or dream among plants and flowers will bless you. A café table can become a wonderful destination for one or two. We set a small table under a five-foot white umbrella near our large white hydrangea in our backyard. It's one of my favorite places to read or work on summer mornings and is a handy overflow dining spot for guests.

If time spent outside would mean melting in the heat or fighting bugs (or if you don't have an outdoor space) bring your efforts inside. Invite in the refreshing benefits of nature with a variety of plants in an assortment of cute pots and baskets.

CREATE A ROMANTIC OUTDOOR DINING ROOM

+ Collect weathered terra-cotta pots and fill them with lavender.

+ Age newer pots by rubbing them with watered-down white paint.

+ Plant fragrant white climbing roses near a trellis.

+ Hang string lights.

+ Set a small table for a quaint dinner party for two.

+ Mix and match vintage or old-world accessories.

+ Add visual texture with items of varying heights such as lanterns, candlesticks, cheese boards, natural linen napkins, and potted herbs.

◇

Taste and see that the Lord is good; blessed is the one who takes refuge in him.

PSALM 34:8

LET'S HAVE A PICNIC!

Summer is all about savoring carefree days and time spent outside. While in the winter months we might eat at the table or gather around a movie, picnics can make mealtimes special when the weather allows.

You don't need anything fancy to set up a backyard dining space. Let nature provide the perfect canopy of stars or sunshine. A checkered blanket on the lawn, a plaid tablecloth on a rickety old picnic table, and a set of Adirondack chairs around a firepit contribute to the carefree mood of a summer evening.

A sturdy basket with a handle can be a charming way to transport snacks to the backyard, a local park, or a sandy beach on a summer evening. Pack a bottle of something sparkling, a healthy salad fresh from the garden or local farm, homemade jam and biscuits, and a tray of sliced fruit, or prepare a hot meal on the grill. It really doesn't matter what you serve, just keep it simple. Abandon expectations of perfection, and know that everyone will savor these moments, now and for years to come.

SUMMER SMOOTHIE BOWL

Make ordinary moments in your day more extraordinary. A smoothie bowl is a simple but healthy morning meal or anytime treat. A few thoughtful ingredients creatively placed can make it a lovely moment to savor in your day. Experiment with a variety of shapes and vibrant colors, and let your inner artist shine.

Try some of these smoothie combinations, or get creative with your own (choose amounts according to your preference):

+ frozen pineapples, mangos, bananas, strawberries, orange juice, a handful of spinach

+ frozen acai puree, apple juice, bananas, strawberries, blueberries

+ cashew or coconut yogurt, peanut butter, pitted dates, cardamom spice, water

+ bananas, almond butter, pitted dates, cinnamon, almond or oat milk

+ frozen blueberries, mangos, almond or oat milk

+ frozen blackberries, mangos, bananas, almond or oat milk

+ frozen peaches, strawberries, coconut yogurt, coconut water

+ frozen bananas, raspberries, pomegranate juice, orange juice, almond or oat milk

+ frozen bananas, pineapple juice, coconut milk, coconut yogurt, raspberries

Topping ideas: fresh sliced fruit (try kiwi slices, bananas, strawberries, raspberries, figs, blackberries, and the like), almonds, cacao nibs, coconut flakes, granola, goji berries, pomegranates, chia seeds, flax seeds, pumpkin seeds, hemp seeds, honey or agave, or cinnamon.

TIPS

Freeze your bowl before assembling your smoothie to slow down the melting process.
Keep bananas on hand for smoothies! They will give a smoothie bowl a thick and creamy texture.
Chop up bananas and keep them in a container in the freezer
so you'll always be prepared to whip up a smoothie.

KEEP A SUMMER SELF-CARE JOURNAL

Select a summer journal to inspire your self-care choices and reflections. Any bound notebook will do (or use my Dwelling Well Journal). This can be a place to keep your seasonal wellness thoughts and record your well-being journey. Your journal can be the personal space where you

+ set intentions to uplift your emotions with positive meditation and habits,

+ gather notes on prayers and gratitude,

+ create a list of favorite activities,

+ chronicle your adventures preparing healthy summer meals,

+ establish your favorite self-care wellness routines, and

+ record your emotions throughout your intentional summer. *How did you feel? What experiences brought you joy?*

At the end of a season, make a list of the activities you wanted to do but didn't (check that bucket list!) so you can fit them in early next summer.

Next summer, flip back to the previous year's pages (do the same in each season). You'll find ideas as you look back at your notes, and when you're down, you can use them to inspire hope and encourage yourself with how far you've come.

FIND JOY IN THE SIMPLE THINGS

Part of what will make your life and home more lovely this summer is rediscovering what is *in front of you*.

Simple joys in our surroundings may not necessarily shout, "Look at me, I'm amazing!" but they quietly *delight* you. Delight is what you feel when something wonderful takes you by surprise. Simplicity is subtle, so the joy found in it can sneak up on you. It's like an unexpected gift you receive only when you are paying attention to how you feel in your surroundings.

Simple joys are magnified by removing what *distracts* and focusing on what *delights* you. Certainly, that could mean simplifying your decor, using a less jarring color palette, or having fewer patterns in a room. It could mean removing clutter or completing unfinished projects that become a distraction or increase stress.

Simple joys are also found in scenes and moments. Think of warm sunshine streaming through a room on a cool morning or the delightful breeze gently billowing curtains through an open window. They can also be discovered through the serenity you feel when your counters are clean or in the deep breath you take after you've decluttered a long-neglected closet.

Even the sound of laughter in the house on a lazy summer day is a reminder that it's not the *material things* we have or add or buy that transform our homes; it's the simple joys that change *us* from the inside out.

CURATE A SIMPLE LIFE

What does a simple life look like for you? Everyone has their own definition of simplicity, of course, but for me, it means I have appropriate margins in my life.

Finding margins in my day means I will carve out time for myself or slow the pace when I become aware that I carry an unnecessary stress load. When I protect the margins in my schedule, I can live more fully in the moments that matter to me.

If I don't have a moment to breathe, or time for daydreaming, solitude, or reflection, that's my cue to pull back on something. A simple life feels like a more balanced life. It doesn't mean that every moment is simple or equally balanced; certainly, we still have stress and hectic schedules in every season. Balance means that if one area of my life must be extra busy, I will need to find other ways to recalibrate for my own well-being.

The more stuff or activities we have in our lives, the more decisions we inadvertently invite into our lives as well. Decisions can become overwhelming and paralyzing when there are too many of them on our plates!

Simplifying life is a process. Commit to making the simplest decisions as often as possible. Avoid rationalizing any decision that makes life more complicated than necessary!

The decisions we make every day set the default habits by which we live. Granted, we don't always have a choice in everything that comes into our lives. How can we begin to live with more intention so we can not only stay afloat in the ebb and flow of each season but live more fully amid the unwelcome interruptions?

Making room for more of our joy-filled, soul-filling habits, daily rhythms, and rituals in this season can protect us from feeling overwhelmed by the frenzy and keep us inspired through the ebb and flow of life.

DELIGHT IN SUMMER PLEASURES

Find beauty in relaxed daily rhythms by carving out more margins in the day to savor the pleasures of summer. Make it a habit to celebrate the little moments this summer, expressing gratitude for all the season offers.

Listen to the laughter of the people you love as they're enjoying a lazy summer day. It's a reminder to be grateful that it's not the material things we have or can buy that transform a home into a welcoming, nurturing place.

+ Savor the taste of fresh watermelon or an ice-cold lemonade.

+ Notice the rays of sunshine cascading into a room during a summer golden hour.

+ Delight in a cool evening breeze.

We may not get a vacation from the never-ending needs of our homes, but look for ways to experience more gratitude amid the routine and upkeep of it all. Pay more attention to the serenity you feel when your kitchen is clean, savor a moment of peace when the laundry is folded, and take a deep breath after you've decluttered a long-neglected closet.

Look for opportunities to be grateful in the ordinary and mundane moments. The more we invite a sense of gratitude and celebration into our daily lives, the more we'll be able to offer to the world around us!

AROMATHERAPY SHOWER SPRAY

Spritz a DIY essential oil spray in your shower to treat yourself to a lovely spa-like experience at home. The natural scents will mix with the steam, diffusing into the air so you can take in the relaxing, mood-lifting benefits. These also make lovely gifts in any season.

+ 4 ounces distilled water

+ 2 ounces witch hazel

+ 25 drops essential oils

+ *Optional:* dried flowers or herbs

Try these variations:

+ Wake up and breathe: Eucalyptus + peppermint + lemon verbena

+ Summer garden: Neroli + ylang-ylang + orange

SUMMER LOVE LETTERS

+ Let someone go in front of you in line.

+ Offer to watch a friend's pets or water plants when they go out of town.

+ Take new coloring books and crayons to a waiting room of a doctor's office or hospital.

+ Handwrite a love note on a travel postcard.

+ Have a family campout in the backyard.

How lovely to think that no one need wait a moment, we can start now, start slowly changing the world!

ANNE FRANK

AUTUMN

— ◇ —

Gratitude unlocks the fullness of life. It turns what we have into enough, and more. It turns denial into acceptance, chaos to order, confusion to clarity. It can turn a meal into a feast, a house into a home, a stranger into a friend. Gratitude makes sense of our past, brings peace for today and creates a vision for tomorrow.

MELODY BEATTIE

RHYTHMS FOR RECONNECTION

Sweater weather is my favorite. From the feel of the crisp air as my legs swing out from under the covers on the first chilly autumn morning to the warmth I feel when I pull on my coziest knit sweater or fuzziest house socks, the senses of this season heighten all of the experiences.

The beauty, sounds, and scents are incorporated into the rhythm of my days, and these moments become embedded into my fondest memories of this cozy season. From the ordinary tasks to the start of holidays and a season of get-togethers, everything that means the most can be elevated and celebrated.

Autumn is the season to reconnect your heart and soul to the familiar pleasures of home and hospitality. It might be a season of loud or quiet, peaceful or wild, happy or less so. My home has grown quieter each fall as my children have flown the nest one by one. I miss the seasons filled with children's voices, back-to-school clothes, backpacks and lunch boxes; they were treasured days. But quiet is nice too.

Honor the season you're in. It's the richness of the memories we make and the gratitude we cultivate in our homes right now that will transform us throughout the seasons.

MAKE AUTUMN LOVELY

20 LITTLE THINGS TO LOOK FORWARD TO

Settle in for a moment of quiet reflection with a cup of tea, a pen, and a notebook. *What are 20 little things you'd like to do or experience this season?* Jot them in your notebook and get them scheduled on your calendar before the season gets away from you.

PLAN AUTUMN RHYTHMS FOR RECONNECTION

HOME*MAKING —Reconnect to the simple pleasures of home-tending.
SOUL*TENDING —Express gratitude and authenticity to fill others and yourself.

GATHER LOVELY LIFE LESSONS

+ Live with grace and gratitude.

+ Grow through the evolving and organic shifts in the beauty around you.

+ Reconnect to your home, traditions, and sense of hospitality as you prepare your nest for celebration and comfort.

HOME*MAKING

Reconnect to the simple pleasures of home-tending

SIMPLE GRACES

Creating a cozy and nurturing environment is a meaningful endeavor. A home is more than just a shelter; it prepares our families to go out into the community to make a difference and graciously invites us in again to reconnect, refuel, and refresh.

We don't have to do everything perfectly. Who really knows how to do it all anyway? Your fall home-tending rhythms and efforts will make life more pleasant, lovely, and memorable. It's a commitment to simple everyday graces that turn a house into a home.

In fall, we crave spaces that are uncluttered by chaos and unnecessary stuff yet still very much full of tangible and intangible comforts. Homemaking isn't just about preparing your home for living; it's about savoring special moments that fill you with more joy.

Whether you're looking forward to spending time in the kitchen baking pumpkin treats or spending a season nesting and making spaces and spots comfier, create a haven that inspires you and your family.

There are many ways to make your home more comfortable, memorable, and personal. Decorate the porch with fall pumpkins to welcome your family home, hang string lights around the door to bring more sparkle to the entry, or paint the table you will gather around for Thanksgiving this year.

Explore what makes you and those you love connect to each other and to the gifts of the season.

DECORATE TO REFLECT YOUR
FAMILY, STYLE, AND STORY

Styles may come and go, but a home should first and foremost be designed for the people who live there.

We are all in unique homes and seasons in life. Searching social media for decorating ideas can be inspirational, but it can also be a trap for creatives and people pleasers alike. The options can be overwhelming and distracting. It can make it difficult to hear your own voice let alone to find your own style. It's helpful to turn inward to create a home that will be meaningful.

Make your home a reflection of your family. Our lives are always evolving. A home should serve as a haven in this time of life. It should speak deeply to your needs. Take a brief inventory:

What type of home do you envision for yourself and your loved ones in this season?

What style or arrangements work for your family and your life? Don't worry about what others think!

Years ago, I started putting up our Christmas tree just before Thanksgiving. I took a bit of flak for it from followers online, but my personal feeling was (and is) that I can be extremely thankful and festive at the same time.

I love sitting down for Thanksgiving dinner with our family next to the twinkling lights of the tree. For me, this atmosphere invites the wonder of Christmas to begin with Thanksgiving. That one simple ritual makes the entire holiday season feel calmer, more relaxing, more intentional, and enjoyable.

I'm definitely a proponent of embracing our family's own style and story regarding how and when we celebrate and decorate, as it makes the holidays so personal and meaningful.

Fall nesting is the enjoyable practice of…
creating a warm and inviting ambience
honoring and practicing comforting rituals
nourishing and gathering the people we love
awakening our senses to savor life
puttering with joy to make spaces cozy
appreciating the season we're in
nurturing contentment in our surroundings

RECONNECT WITH GRATITUDE

Those of us with house-shaped hearts long to feel a deep connection to whatever home we live in. Dwelling on the desire for a house you don't, can't, or may never have will create discontentment, but some elbow grease, a bit of serendipity, and gratitude can turn the house you have into the dream house you hold in your heart.

It doesn't take much to add a personal, seasonal touch and welcome yourself home with gratitude.

+ Move an accessory to a new place.

+ Swap out art for something different or seasonal.

+ Choose one or two seasonal colors to mix into your decor with textiles.

+ Rearrange the furniture to bring pieces closer and make rooms cozier.

Let us not become weary in doing good, for at the proper time we will
reap a harvest if we do not give up.

GALATIANS 6:9

A WELCOMING DOOR BASKET

Placing a basket on the front door is a simple way to have an ever-evolving seasonal or celebrative display. Here are some ideas to get your door decor welcome-ready.

+ You can fill the basket with fresh blooms or small potted plants (use a vase or florist foam in the basket, lined with a plastic bag to keep dirt and water in). If you don't want to deal with real plants, use any of the beautiful faux foliage options.

+ Tie a pretty ribbon around the basket or handle.

+ Add ornaments, banners, or flags.

+ Honor birthdays, holidays, weddings, or baby showers with colorful streamers or blooms.

+ Hang small signs with wire looped through the front or base of the basket.

+ Drape or wrap twinkle lights (every season is right for battery-run lights).

Let yourself be creative. When you are deciding how to spruce up your door each month or season, think about guests who may come by and also think about what will bring a smile or a rush of happiness to you and your family each time you enter your home.

COLLECT THE PRETTY AND PRACTICAL

It isn't the things we've collected that make our lives rich and meaningful; it's the people and memories we hold dear. Yet day-to-day life at home involves all kinds of activities and upkeep, so why not make everything we use more lovely and meaningful?

I don't necessarily think of myself as a collector, but I do like to have tools and accessories in my kitchen that are pretty and practical. The pieces we collect are used and loved. They have become a part of our family's history, connecting each home and season to the present.

Our collection of copper pots was built over time. One by one, these treasures were found at estate and garage sales. They were used for cooking or hung on walls to decorate our various homes. We collected cookie cutters for holiday baking with the kids; they bring back so many memories. Even my trusty 30-year-old KitchenAid stand mixer has a lifetime of stories to tell. It's been with us since my kids were little enough to lick the beaters. (Cue all the tears!)

My favorite accessories are our collection of beautiful wooden spoons. The day we moved into our very first home as a young married couple, I set a crock on my counter to hold my wood spoons. I knew wood utensils would serve a purpose. Not only were they useful to stir the soup and add texture to our kitchen, but they became a part of our everyday experiences and stories.

My current collection is brimming with gorgeous hand-carved wood utensils gathered and gifted to me over the years.

There is something so special in *investing in* quality or sentimental pieces that will not only stand the test of time but also become a cherished part of our family's day-to-day life and history.

CREATE AN INTENTIONAL FEELING OF HOME

The feeling of our homes has a powerful impact on our lives and souls. The home is such a sacred space. We are most at peace in it when we have eliminated the excess distractions and are still surrounded by the things we love.

The decisions in our homes should be intentional. Whether we are choosing what we want to keep or remove from our surroundings, or how we want to care for the spaces we live in, we are cultivating a mood and designing the experiences of our lives.

Are you surrounded by things that impact you in positive ways?

Is what you have in your home beautiful and useful to you or your family?

Look at your spaces and how they are used. For example, think through the main reasons your family is coming and going through your entryway (for school, work, and other activities). How can that area be streamlined and organized to best serve these needs?

Go to your dining area. Think through who you will be hosting and serving there this season. How could your dining spaces be set up and hospitality supplies be freshened to make this space feel more welcoming this season?

As you declutter or rearrange spaces with intention, focus your mind on how a surface or corner will feel so much cozier and more inviting when you are finished. How might you be able to beautify this space so you'd enjoy it even more?

RITUALS FOR A TIDIER AUTUMN HOME

There can be so much more satisfaction in home-keeping when we make the mood and the pressure light. Make the process enjoyable with simple, doable rituals.

Create your autumn soundtrack for tidying. This will inspire you and the atmosphere of your home! Do you want to motivate your child to help you clean? Let them choose the songs and set the background music for your day of making your home lovelier.

Incorporate the one-minute rule. If you can put it away in less than a minute, do it. Don't walk on by or set it somewhere else; that only multiplies the mess and creates more work for yourself. Deal with it swiftly and move on!

Give away what you don't want, need, or use. Thrift stores are your friend. Gather up everything you don't need in this season and bless someone else with it. If you are struggling to decide what to let go of, try this rule: If it could be replaced easily and affordably in the future, out it goes! Chances are you'll never miss it.

Do a surface sweep. Run through a room in the house and pick up everything on horizontal surfaces. You'll feel so much more inspired to make your home festive and cozy once there's room for seasonal things you love. Also, take time to go through the items you removed from the surfaces and evaluate which to keep and which to add to your giveaway box.

SEVEN WAYS TO MAKE
YOUR FIREPLACE COZIER

If you are lucky enough to have a fireplace or stove, turn it into a retreat space in your home. Let it soothe you and provide you with visual and physical warmth.

1. Pull comfortable chairs in a little closer to the fireplace to create a cozy focal point.

2. Add a rug for softness. (Not close enough to be a fire hazard, of course! Safety first.)

3. Set up a basket for books and a comfortable footstool nearby so you can put your feet up!

4. Make sure you have your fireplace tools ready if you have a wood-burning fireplace.

5. Even if you don't use your fireplace to burn fires, you can still decorate it with birch logs, battery-operated string lights, or candles for ambience.

6. Add a log holder next to the fireplace for convenience and character.

7. Decorate your mantel for fall. Branches, pumpkins, wheat, eucalyptus, framed art, flowers, candles…whatever inspires you!

TEND TO THE HEART OF THE HOME

The kitchen is the heart of the home. Practice daily habits there with care and intention. What are your favorite autumn memories in the kitchen?

My plan is to have my dishwasher loaded and sink empty and clean before I go to bed. Sometimes it has felt like a lofty goal, but waking up with a clean kitchen makes such a difference in how I feel and what I accomplish during the day.

Here are simple secrets to keep the heart of your home a happy, welcoming place:

+ Clean as you go whenever possible. It will make a world of difference in your day and your evening.

+ Use the pretty dishes. It's far more motivating to have your pretty dishes clean and stacked in the cabinet ready to enjoy rather than to see them piled high in a sink covered in leftover lasagna!

+ Pour yourself a cuppa—something comforting to sip as you clean—or prepare one to savor as a reward as soon as the kitchen is clean.

+ Turn on your favorite music, audiobook, or podcast to enhance the cleaning experience.

+ Decorate for the season. A bowl of gourds on the counter, a flickering candle, a vase of sunflowers on the table, or a pretty fall hand towel will make the kitchen feel extra cozy and inviting when the sink is clean!

+ Combine a few favorite autumn essential oils with a toxin-free household cleaner to make sink scrubbing smell more festive!

+ Polish the sink when you're finished. I keep a small dry rag under the sink to make it quick and easy to polish up the sink. A shiny sink will make you feel extra cheerful in the morning.

ENJOY A CLEAN AND PRETTY PANTRY

The visual appeal of your pantry will increase tenfold with this easy process. Don't tackle the entire pantry all at once—focus on prettifying one shelf or drawer at a time. Then when you have time while dinner is cooking or during a break in your workday, you can transform one more area or shelf. Set a timer and make simple improvements.

+ Choose a shelf, drawer, or corner to improve.

+ Remove everything.

+ Clean.

+ Return what you want to keep.

+ Dust off cans and jars so they shine.

+ Group and stack like items together.

+ Turn all labels in the same direction to make your eyes happy.

+ Have fun with a label maker.

+ Look for baskets or pretty containers to corral wayward items.

Much better!

A COZY SIMMER POT

It's time to celebrate all things cozy, and there's nothing that will make your house smell more like autumn than a simmer pot bubbling on the stove.

Make a simmer pot when you're enjoying seasonal fun like carving pumpkins with the kids or even to elevate the experience of ordinary fall tasks. Cleaning? Put a simmer pot on the stove to make tidying up more enjoyable. Raking leaves? Set up a Crock-Pot to fill the house with a warm spicy aroma when you come back in.

+ 2 navel oranges, sliced with peels

+ 1 apple, sliced

+ 4 cinnamon sticks

+ 3 star anise

+ 1 tsp. cardamom

+ 1 tsp. whole cloves

+ 1½ tsp. vanilla extract

+ 5 cups water (Crock-Pot or on the stove)

You can also add pomegranates or pears for a fun twist.

DESIGNATE A HOME BASE

When students return to school in the fall, the rest of us also return to more structure and routine in our lives and work. Whether you have a home-based business or you simply want to be intentional with your time, it's helpful to set up a designated spot for doing activities that are important to you.

One season, I decided I no longer needed a desk or designated office. I'd been a home entrepreneur for over a decade, and with laptop computers and cell phones, I reasoned I would be fine to work in the living room, a coffee shop, or from my bed if I wanted!

However, in a few months, I was struggling with boundaries, time management, and focus. I'm a free spirit in many ways, yet I thrive when I know exactly what to do next and where to go. The experiment was worthwhile because I understood how important a designated work area is for my sanity.

I took the leap and claimed the TV room that is rarely used now that my children are grown. Initially, it felt like a selfish splurge because I've had seasons when the only quiet spot I could claim was a closet. But a home is meant to serve and inspire our families *and* ourselves. Admitting my needs brought so much peace to me and eventually to our home as well.

Every home will have its own limitations, and every season will present a new need. How could you utilize the space you have for your needs right now?

Have regular hours for work and play; make each day both useful and pleasant, and prove that you understand the worth of time by employing it well. Then youth will be delightful, old age will bring few regrets, and life will become a beautiful success.

LOUISA MAY ALCOTT

that house was...'a perfect house,
whether you like food or sleep,
or story-telling or singing, or just
sitting and thinking best,
or a pleasant mixture of them all'.
Merely to be there
was a cure for weariness,
fear, and sadness.
J.R.R. TOLKIEN

OUR HOMES SHOULD
inspire us
TO GO OUT
INTO THE WORLD
TO DO GREAT THINGS
& THEN *welcome* US BACK
FOR
refreshment

Romans 12:9-10

Love must be sincere. Hate what is evil;
cling to what is good.
Be devoted to one another in brotherly love.
one another above yourselves.

I WILL GIVE THANKS TO YOU, LORD WITH ALL MY HEART
Psalm 9:1

CULTIVATE GRATITUDE IN EVERY ROOM

We'll feel more inspired to create a meaningful atmosphere if we focus on celebrating ordinary moments with more gratitude.

In our fast-paced culture here in the United States, we always seem to cram a lot into a short period of time. A desire for instant gratification and being under the constant pressure of so many expectations on our time can cause us to feel frustration for everything and everyone in our way. We can nearly forget how it feels to take a deep breath and savor the season we're in, let alone how to express deep gratitude for the good already present in our lives.

To cultivate a true and lasting spirit of gratitude, we have to learn to dwell on blessings daily. Here are three practical gratitude rituals I began practicing in my home years ago; they transformed my own attitude toward each person and room in my home.

1. *Gratitude in the kitchen.* The process of cleaning a house and fixing meals can feel like an endless loop. But instead of feeling overwhelmed by the regularity of chores, we can refocus our hearts to practice gratitude for the gift of having a home to care for.

   The kitchen has traditionally been considered an area where nurturing takes place, so as we prepare food, clean counters, and empty the sink each day, we can be reminded that the joy and tender care we show in taking care of this space will establish an atmosphere of gratefulness, grace, and love.

2. *Thankfulness in the dining room.* Is your dining table covered with papers and clutter every day? Establish a daily practice of thankfulness by creating an inviting gathering space. When we treasure our gifts, we take care of them, so be inspired to see this table as a sacred space for blessing your loved ones.

Corral all the clutter in the basket and let everyone pick out his or her own stuff to put away. Wipe the table so you have a clean surface. If you have kids, they can help make a centerpiece out of seasonal elements. Arrange candles or string lights on the table to set the mood as everyone sits down. It doesn't have to be perfect; just have fun with this ritual every night leading up to Thanksgiving (and make it a habit that will stick with you long after the holidays). Take a moment to look at each face around the table and thank God for them.

3. *Grace in the living room.* Whether you have kids, roommates, dogs, or a husband, it's easy to get frustrated by the mess others make in your space. Use this season to practice a new habit of looking for opportunities to be grateful for the people right there on your couch!

At the end of the day, when everyone is tired and the upkeep of the house is spiraling out of control, take a deep breath and offer grace instead of griping. Say a prayer of gratitude for the mess-makers in your living room. Gratitude won't necessarily solve the mess at that moment, but it can slow the pace and soften your heart and remind you that there is still so much to be grateful for.

Gratefulness isn't hard. Forgetting to be grateful is what makes it hard.

ANN VOSKAMP

SOUL * TENDING

*Express gratitude and authenticity
to fill others and yourself*

SEASONAL RHYTHMS FOR BODY,
MIND, AND SOUL

There's an ever-evolving kaleidoscope of flowers and plants around our yard; each season reveals its purpose and displays its beauty in rhythms. With a steaming hot mug of coffee in hand, I savor the glow of the autumn sun rising and the early morning drops of dew on my hydrangeas. The bright, cheerful blooms and foliage in summer hues quietly and gracefully begin to fade into deep autumn shades of corals, moody pinks, greens, and maroons. They are magnificent in summer but also gloriously beautiful in autumn.

A time for letting go, resting, renewal, planning, planting seeds, budding, growing, flourishing—each season offers us lovely and meaningful gifts. By honoring the pace and rhythm of nature in your life, more beauty and grace are added to the whole of your own well-being.

Unlike our endless to-do lists or daily and monthly schedules that can become overshadowed by responsibility or obligations, seasonal rhythms invite us to slow down and live more mindfully within the ebb and flow of how we feel, grow, and flourish.

Fitting all our needs and personal expectations into the confines of a day often feels futile, but seasonal rhythms will free us to focus on various aspects of our well-being throughout the year. We can discover our own organic and creative approaches to nurture our faith and care for our bodies, minds, and souls through the benefits and gifts of every season.

CREATE A QUIET CORNER

I've always found creating a cozy corner in my home to be beneficial to my well-being, particularly when it's used as an intentional spot for prayer and quiet time.

When my kids were young, I had a pink chair in the corner of my bedroom where I could sit for a moment to myself. It wasn't easy to take the time to actually use it once the day got started, but I found that just seeing the corner set up and ready across from me as I woke up became my gentle nudge to get out of bed a few minutes early.

To this day, having a designated area of my home set up for any intentional purpose inspires me to actually do the things I say I want to do!

Pick your coziest, comfiest chair. Whether it's a chair in the corner of your bedroom or by the fireplace, a comfortable spot will invite you to enjoy a morning quiet time routine.

Select a favorite morning mug. I don't like to just chug coffee on the run. I prefer to savor it as a part of my morning ritual. Pick a mug for your coffee or tea that feels just right in your hands, something pretty or seasonal to enhance the whole experience.

Grab a charming little stool or table. Set it by your chair. It will be handy for holding a journal, book, or mug as you get comfy in your spot.

Toss on a throw blanket. I mean, is it even cozy if you don't have a blanket? Even if it's still a bit too warm to curl up in a blanket, it will add a textural element that will give it added style and interest.

Add a basket of inspiration. Corral your quiet time supplies—such as a journal, a notebook, a devotional, a book you're reading, headphones if you like to listen to music or podcasts, scented oils and a diffuser, and a set of your favorite pens—in a basket nearby so you're ready to dive in and make the most of your time!

Place a plant nearby. Refresh your cozy corner. A plant adds a finishing touch and a sense of life to space, even in a season where we might not have fresh flowers.

When you recognize the festive and the still moments as moments of prayer, then you gradually realize that to pray is to live.

HENRI NOUWEN

SAVOR SEASONAL DELIGHTS (THINK PIE!)

If you live near a farm, apple orchard, or farmer's market, autumn is the time to take a field trip! Make it a fun autumn tradition. Invite your friends or family to join you. When my kids were little, we loved our annual excursions to the local farm. We'd take a hayride, go through the maze, visit the animals, and of course, pick out our pumpkins and grab fresh apples too.

Honeycrisp, Pink Lady—do you have a favorite? What better way to use your freshly picked apples than to bake an autumn or Thanksgiving pie! I used to think baking a pie from scratch was a lot of trouble. Sure, I loved it when *other people* made homemade pies so I could enjoy them. Of course, I made meals from scratch and even my own applesauce, but something about piecrust, especially when we became gluten-free, seemed like too much effort.

My thoughts on the joy of pie-making changed a few years ago when my daughter Courtney began baking pies from scratch. She turned pie-making into an experience. Her pies are works of art with darling seasonal shapes cut out of dough creatively placed on top. And they are definitely more delicious than any store-bought pie.

Simple pleasures don't have to be fast or even *simple* to make life lovelier. In fact, quite often the lovely life is about slowing down to savor fewer experiences more. It's not just about the joy of tasting the first or last bite of hot apple pie (dripping with vanilla ice cream, of course) but the experience of baking the pie with love and care. Pie-making can be an intentional simple pleasure. It just requires time, planning, and effort...and is worth every minute!

PRETTIFY THOSE PIES

Pie doesn't have to be a work of art to be enjoyed, but we've found that even as novice pie-makers, there are simple ways to elevate its look or give it a seasonal flair.

Create a Lattice Pattern

Roll out pie dough with a rolling pin, and use a pizza cutter to cut out several long, rectangular, one-inch-wide strips. Carefully lift and place the strips over the pie filling, about an inch or so apart. Use longer strips for the center of the pie and shorter strips for the sides.

For a true woven lattice pattern, you can pull the vertical strips back one by one, and weave horizontal strips alternately above and below each vertical strip.

Get Fancy

+ Turn a basic pie into a bakery-window-worthy prize with decorative piecrust shapes. Use cookie cutters to create lovely shapes and designs.

We have found that spring-loaded piecrust stamps work well to cut and emboss, plus they have a plunger to easily eject them.

+ Press firmly on the plunger, let go, lift, and drop them into your hand before arranging on the pie.

+ Just before baking, use a silicone brush to add an egg wash or melted coconut oil.

+ Sprinkle brown sugar on top before placing the pie in the oven.

+ Punch out several extra piecrust shapes and bake them separately. You'll be set if you need to replace any that break while baking, and you'll be very glad if there are extras to savor like cookies. So good.

TIP

If your dough is more fragile, like the gluten-free dough we make, create a faux lattice design to reduce handling. Simply place piecrust strips horizontally on top of vertically placed strips.

DECORATE FOR OCCASIONS

You can make a pie for any holiday, special occasion, to welcome a new neighbor, to celebrate a friend, or just because!

+ Cut out shapes, letters, or a combination to create personalized pies all year long.

+ Easter pie—eggs, bunnies, flowers, crosses, and so on

+ flower-power pie—flower shapes, such as daisies, tulips, sunflowers

+ love or Valentine's Day pie—hearts or *x*'s and *o*'s

+ Fourth of July—stars, stripes

+ birthdays—letters for a name, or the shape of something the honoree loves

+ autumn and Thanksgiving—leaves, apples, pumpkins

+ winter and Christmas—snowflakes, snow people, bows, trees, stars

Arrange the shapes all over the pie, layer them, or simply place them around the edges. A single shape in the middle of the pie is also beautiful.

EXTEND AUTHENTIC HOSPITALITY

Crisp breezes can inspire more than just a sweater-wearing afternoon and an autumn trip to the pumpkin patch. This season can inspire us to invite friends into the comfort of our homes for fun and holiday festivities!

Gratefully, we can dismiss the notion that to open our homes, we first need to have everything perfect. If we wait until everything is perfect, we'll never open our doors. Authenticity is so much more endearing.

With that said, there doesn't need to be laundry out on the table during the dinner party to ensure everyone knows you're authentic. What matters in hospitality isn't measured by our houses' state or the visibility of our laundry piles; it's about the connections we make with others as our truest selves. We are not inauthentic if we are being the type of hostess we want to be.

One fall, my husband and I were invited by new friends to visit them and see the old house they had moved into and were remodeling. While we would have thoroughly enjoyed being served crackers on paper plates, we were greeted with a lovingly prepared gourmet meal fit for royalty. Sure, there were probably moving boxes, partially furnished rooms, paint cans, and incomplete projects everywhere, but that's not what we noticed. Their home's welcoming atmosphere and their heartfelt hospitality, the delicious food, and the genuine conversation are what made a lasting impression on us.

They didn't do any of it to impress us; they did it to show kindness and connect with us in their authentic way. When we left that day, we were grateful they didn't wait for ideal circumstances to open their door. We were touched not only because they invited us into their home but also because they opened their hearts to welcome us into their lives.

The way you welcome others into your home should be authentic to you; after all, you're inviting others into *your* home! If you are a spur-of-the-moment pizza night kind of gal, your friends will love you for including them in your spontaneity. If you love to celebrate life by setting out a pretty new welcome mat and inviting others to enjoy a special evening in your home, do it! Allow your hospitality style to be a reflection of you so you are inspired to extend invitations and open your doors. When you are fully yourself, you'll relax and be comfortable, and others will be too.

HOST A FRIENDSGIVING

A Friendsgiving is a gathering of friends who come together to enjoy a large meal in the spirit of Thanksgiving. These are wonderful to host or attend at any time of year. But what a great way to experience deeper community during the holidays, which can be either a lonely time of year for some or seasons of frenzy.

Create a space and an experience that extends peace and hospitality. Here are five tips for hosting your circle of friends:

1. *Plan the meal.* If you don't want to shoulder preparing the entire meal yourself, make it a potluck! Ask everyone to bring their favorite dish, or divide everyone into categories like vegetables, side dishes, and desserts so there won't be many duplicates. Be aware of any food preferences, allergies, or sensitivities so no one will go home hungry! Or host a fall harvest party with pumpkin treats and cider to keep it even simpler.

2. *Think through the logistics.* Where will you serve the food, and where will people sit? If you set up those two areas and plan out related serving pieces, you'll feel less frazzled.

3. *Ask for the support you need.* Could you use help setting up tables, doing dishes, or planning activities? Do you need extra chairs or silverware? Give others a chance to be a part of the day's festivities.

4. *Set a lovely mood.* Keep it simple. Make your front porch welcoming with candles or string lights. Have soft background music, and set small gourds or pumpkins across the table.

5. *Make everyone feel welcome.* Plan out a few fun conversation starters for guests who are not well acquainted with each other. If you're gathering a group of old friends, plan out a time to express gratitude for each other and reminisce about your friendship.

EMBRACE GRATITUDE RITUALS

Becoming grateful for your whole life involves seeing the blessings, the comforts, the people, and the beauty around you. Start noticing those today and turn a simple exercise into habits of thanksgiving.

+ Make a list of ten things about your home and your life you are thankful for.

+ Write a note to someone you care about, listing five things you love about them.

+ Bundle up and take a walk through a park.

+ Make note of three natural elements you find beautiful, even in the winter.

+ Volunteer to serve the needs of someone else without any expectation of receiving something in return.

+ Make a list of ten things you're grateful for that may not always be at the top of your list.

AUTUMN LOVE LETTERS

+ Give a special gift to a teacher.

+ Offer to babysit for a friend.

+ Put a kind note on someone's windshield.

+ Ask a cashier how their day is going.

+ Make a family fort in the living room and watch a movie on a laptop.

No act of kindness, no matter how small, is ever wasted.

AESOP

WINTER

⬦

*I wonder if the snow loves the trees and fields, that it
kisses them so gently? And then it covers them up snug,
you know, with a white quilt; and perhaps it says,
"Go to sleep, darlings, till the summer comes again."*

LEWIS CARROLL, *THROUGH THE LOOKING-GLASS*

RHYTHMS
FOR REST

Waking up on a winter morning conjures up all kinds of feelings for me. The uncelebrated days, tucked between the delight of the holidays and the anticipation of spring, wear on my joy-levels.

While I would love a tropical, sunny vacation destination when fall fades away, it's not often an option for us. Wintering at home it is! I make the most of it by embracing my home as a calm retreat for rest in a blustery storm. And I look for the blessings.

We think we lack enough hours in a day to do everything we want to do, but what we need is more hours to do less. Short winter days might be exactly the gift we need. With less daylight for the hustle and bustle of activity, we can savor the downtime of longer winter evenings of quiet activity and reflection.

Winter has become a soul-filling season I truly can enjoy and even look forward to. A peaceful home and a quieter, more restful state of being speaks to me, especially as an introverted homebody.

Maybe you're an extrovert. Or you're blessed to live in a part of the world where the sun shines all winter long (lucky you). Align with winter rhythms and activities that serve your sense of balance. What will speak to your most authentic self? Every season can serve a unique purpose, so reflect on how you might use this season to impact your life and family in all the best ways.

MAKE WINTER LOVELY

20 LITTLE THINGS TO LOOK FORWARD TO

Winter might feel isolating at times, but this quieter season offers treasures. Create your own winter wonderland of rest and surprising connection. If you set aside several hours for yourself each week, what activities or hobbies will bring you joy? What do you want to cook? What games do you want to play? What memories do you want to make? Grab a winter notebook. *What are 20 little things you'd like to do or experience this season?*

PLAN AUTUMN RHYTHMS FOR RECONNECTION

HOME*MAKING —Enjoy the restful rhythms of caring for your sanctuary.
SOUL*TENDING —Make room for soul-filling joys, beauty, and people.

GATHER LOVELY LIFE LESSONS

+ Let this be a slow season with more rest, less stress.

+ Remember to make room for a more soul-filling life.

+ Make your home a cozy sanctuary that nurtures you and others.

HOME*MAKING

Enjoy the restful rhythms of caring for your sanctuary

WELCOME YOURSELF HOME IN WINTER

When we first saw the real estate photos of what would eventually become our home, it didn't feel like the house of my dreams at all. It's not that it didn't have redeeming features; it just wasn't at all the fairy-tale-style of home I dreamed about. Finding a home in Seattle in our price range had proven to be even more challenging than I had expected it to be, so I had to let go of some expectations.

A little more than a year after we moved into our home, our yard was blanketed by several feet of fluffy snow one December eve. It was an unexpected but beautiful sight to wake up to; we don't normally get so much snow on the ground in the Northwest!

As I looked out my kitchen window that morning, it looked like a fairy tale! I thought it must just be the fresh white paint on the house and the green wreaths on the shed surrounded by all the white snow that made it feel so magical. But it was more than that. Those feelings came from a deep sense of love and gratitude for our home. We had been given everything we needed all along.

This home had been an unexpected blessing to us when we first saw it as a 1950s orange-brick ranch house (with lumpy grass from the moles who tunneled through the yard) just as it was a gift to us in that fairy-tale winter moment, with the twinkling lights, white paint, and glistening snow.

The Pepto-Bismol pink sink in my dated bathroom was just as much of a gift to be grateful for as the shiny new porcelain sink I'd be washing dishes in once our kitchen remodel was complete. The gratitude that welled up in me wasn't about project status or things being perfect; I was deeply thankful then and now for the gift of home.

Some people move into the house of their dreams. Others have the opportunity to design a home that fulfills their dreams. And some of us stumble into our dream homes by creating something beautiful and attainable with what we have right in front of us.

DISCOVER PEACE IN HOME RITUALS

Taking care of our winter homes is not just about caring for our physical surroundings. It is about cultivating a mindset of contentment and finding a rhythm of living that leads to more peace and tranquility in mind, body, and spirit.

Make home-keeping a nurturing experience. The daily ritual of cleaning can be a comforting activity and nurturing experience! On cold nights when the kitchen is still warm from cooking (or while you're baking something yummy!), turn on a lamp or a few candles and string lights so the mood is extra cozy while you do the dishes and polish up the sink.

Pair less-fun tasks with happy ones. As you finish your nightly kitchen cleanup, find a pretty container to hold your spatulas, utensils, or baking supplies, or reorganize a drawer with pretty little bowls, trays, or baskets.

Make your bed every morning. It's tempting to leave the bed unmade so you can hop back in for a nap on a chilly day. However, adopting this habit will boost your mood for the entire day. If you like to check off boxes, this practice gives you a sense of accomplishment right away. And you're doing yourself a favor for the whole day.

Make your bed so you will...
start the day off right
keep your sanctuary fresh and welcoming
crawl into bed with joy every evening
sleep better at night
begin and end your day with peace

THREE WAYS TO INSPIRE YOUR KITCHEN

The weather outside is frightful…make the kitchen more delightful!

1. *Tidy and create order.* Kitchens become cluttered over time by the accumulation of forgettable or regrettable little gadgets, small appliances, or barely used packaged food. Daily meal prep is frustrating when you can't find what you need. Go through your pantry, refrigerator, and those barely reachable top cabinets and toss what you rarely use.

   Bring in pretty containers to group like items. Buy new or used pretty bowls, trays, or baskets. Restock your pantry with cold-weather favorites. Now you have more room to prepare comforting meals and for your family to make their own snacks and lunches too.

2. *Nourish yourself and your family.* Preparing a good meal is a wonderful winter activity. Plan in advance to help you choose food that makes you feel great. Stock up on healthy go-to staples you enjoy so you're more likely to cook a nourishing meal at home than to resort to takeout or fast food!

   What gives you the warm fuzzies? Do you love to make a special soup or a hearty hot breakfast? Spend an evening with a good cookbook and a notepad for your shopping list.

3. *Warm up the cold surfaces.* Clean and serene surfaces don't have to feel cold and bare. Add intentional layers to warm them up. Rugs will quiet the room and keep feet toastier. Simple wood or woven accessories such as cutting boards and baskets can create a warmer, homier vibe.

   Beautiful, meaningful objects comfort the heart and home. Pretty dishes or special kitchen accessories can inspire your winter rituals. Add a copper French press to your morning routine, a lovely tea kettle for an afternoon break, or a new soup tureen. What textures, items, or collections will grace your kitchen space this season?

SHINY SINK SCRUB

Clean and pretty surfaces make it a pleasure to come into our kitchen spaces. The scent of this homemade scrub might turn an avoided chore into one of your favorite activities. At the very least, it will help you pause and appreciate the simple beauty of a cared-for, clean home.

+ ½ cup baking soda

+ 5 drops lemon essential oil

+ 5 drops clove essential oil

Mix in a small jar. To use, sprinkle mixture in a wet sink. Top with a capful of a natural household cleaner or a squirt of dish soap. Scrub with a brush and let sit 30 minutes before rinsing.

EDIT YOUR RESTING SPACE

In the busyness of life, we can become accustomed to a frantic existence. Checking email, watching the news, rushing on to the next thing like it's the most urgent priority. But when we enter our bedrooms, we should feel like we step into another world, a place where we can get away from it all. We need a place to be fully refreshed and guarded against the stress of life. A place where we can rest and disconnect from the outside world.

We spend more time in this room than in any other. Rather than allowing it to be the most neglected space in our homes, we can care for it and create surroundings that positively impact our lives and our sleep. Our bedrooms should be a sacred and private refuge within the sanctuary of our homes. It should be a place where we can curl up among our comfiest pillows and let the stressors of our days be exhaled.

To create that refuge, make a winter edit one of your first activities to begin the season. Begin eliminating any visible elements that no longer serve you or do not bring beauty to your life. Remove what makes you feel unsettled or overwhelmed. Decor, clutter, paperwork, laundry, computers, electronics—what's currently in your room? Declutter your surfaces so they are simplified, relaxing, and inspiring. Set aside time to clean out drawers and closets so everything feels useful, tidy, and calming.

Once the room is cleaned and edited for the season, you can carefully layer in whatever comfort elements will enhance your sense of peace and solitude. The fabrics, colors, decor, mood, scents, and lighting can all be chosen with care for their value in the room and your well-being.

HOW TO LAYER YOUR WINTER BED

As you select bedding, play with a variety of cozy textures, or layer on additional patterns and colors to suit your winter style!

+ Start with a fitted sheet (I prefer organic materials—try flannel for maximum coziness).

+ Lay your flat sheet across the bed wrong side up, tucking it in around the foot of the bed.

+ Leave enough length to fold the top sheet down over your comforter as a pretty finishing detail.

+ Layer a soft thick blanket over the top sheet for extra warmth and tuck it in with the sheet.

+ Add a comforter or quilt.

+ Add Euro and or standard shams at the head of the bed (place your nighttime pillows behind the shams or put them in a closet or basket nearby).

+ Place decorative pillows in wintery colors and patterns in front of the shams.

+ Fold a fluffy comforter or duvet in thirds and place it at the end of the bed.

+ Layer a finishing knit or cozy throw blanket on the foot of the bed for more texture.

+ In a guest bedroom, add a breakfast tray as a finishing accessory layer. Have one for your room too so you can curl up in bed with your morning coffee.

PUTTERING TO ENJOY YOUR HOME

If you tend to be a perfectionist or a procrastinator, those habits can complicate your life and your love for your home. They can also hold you back from nesting and enjoying the beauty of the season. That's why I love puttering! It's a reset for my mind and a fresh start to the season.

By definition, to putter is to occupy yourself in an unhurried, pleasant manner on several small tasks or pleasures around the home while not concentrating on anything in particular.

Permit yourself to take a day to putter around the house and note what you're thankful for and what can be improved with one or two actions. Sometimes you inadvertently accomplish something significant while puttering, but that's not the goal. My main objective is to slow my pace as I reset my perspective. Wandering room to room to appreciate my spaces revives my spirits. I feel more joy in my heart and surroundings.

Puttering and paying attention will help you to be present in your home and nurture greater contentment as you understand your role as keeper of the surroundings that impact your mood and inspire you to make everything around you lovely in time.

What I love most about puttering? It feels like a treasure hunt for simple joys. It revives your connection to your home and inspires gratitude as you consider the ways you can make the most of winter to honor your current season of life and your dwelling.

LET THERE BE LOVELY LIGHT

The comfort level of each room becomes more meaningful to our well-being in the winter because we tend to be inside more to observe and obsess over what is wrong. Instead of focusing on the flaws in a home, let's focus on the *feeling* we want to create.

Winter homes will feel moodier due to the limited light outside. But flipping the switch on a sea of overhead lights isn't going to make any space more inviting, so increase light in other ways to boost, not bust, the cozy and happy moods.

Add more natural light. Inspire your spaces with more light from Mother Nature. A friend of mine added a skylight that brought in more sunshine and allowed her to enjoy watching the clouds overhead. Open drapes and even doors between rooms to allow daylight to flow freely.

Mirror the light. Most of us can't change our views or add more windows. Consider using strategically placed mirrors to expand any light and reflect the view out any window.

Bring in more sources. A good guideline is to have at least three light sources in every room. Use a mix of table lamps, floor lamps, task lamps, and overhead lighting. Consider using warmer lightbulbs for the coziest ambience. A favorite lamp is always on my kitchen counter to warm the style and mood of the space. Try it! Lamps can become a statement piece, so find one that adds character.

Choose romantic light. Set the mood to cozy and romantic. One of my winter evening rituals is to walk around the house and turn on all the lamps and sconces. I turn down any ceiling lights so the room is aglow with ambience you'd imagine being in the candlelit homes of yesteryear.

We have wall sconces wired into our kitchen that envelope the room in a soft glow. In several rooms and on our porch, we hung nonelectrical wall sconces and battery-operated candles that have "flames" that flicker. With the click of a remote, the mood goes from dreary to lovely. Honestly, I don't even save them for nighttime; even on a cloudy winter day, the flickering light is so cozy!

MAKE YOUR HOME HOMIER

Life is always lovelier when you truly feel at home. The more personal your choices, the more at-home you and your family will feel. Warm up your spaces with beauty and ease by adding…

+ layers of winter linens on tables

+ faux fur and knit pillows to the sofa

+ draped plaid scarves or throws to the backs of chairs

+ blankets in a basket

+ wood accessories

+ natural winter decor—like oranges, cranberries, evergreen boughs, and pine cones

+ curtains on windows and even interior doors

+ table and floor runners and area rugs

+ winter-themed books in stacks by the fireplace and beds

+ groupings of candles on mantels and dressers

+ comfy furniture so you can curl up

+ special family photos that highlight the season or any happy times

+ framed inspirational quotes

+ vintage accessories and furniture

+ original art from outside artists or your young artists in residence

+ knit blankets stacked on shelves for texture, beauty, and function

Your Christmas decorating choices can be personal too. Don't worry about trends unless there is one that suits your style. I keep my holiday decor simple. That's what I love most. I'm a fan of using what you have for the season's simplicity, memories, and affordability. We mostly use greenery in the form of trees, swags, and wreaths and add in a few favorite whimsical ornaments.

I've referred to our family's holiday decorating style as Forest and Sea for many years because that combination reflects our natural surroundings in the Northwest and encompasses two elements that have become a part of our history as a family. This theme helps me shift toward a holiday mood while preserving the look and feel we find most restful and inspiring.

SOUL*TENDING
Make room for soul-filling joys, beauty, and people

A SOULFUL START TO THE DAY

On the dark and cold mornings of winter, it's tempting to let myself doze in and out of consciousness or grab my phone and connect to the world while staying wrapped in the blankets as long as possible. To get my feet on the floor, I need special winter rituals that gently inspire me to get the day started earlier.

Warm slippers by my bedside and a big knit sweater folded and ready on the bench across from me became a part of my nightly rituals, preparing me in advance to feel cared for and ready for a more comfortable morning. I add these happy layers first thing.

Next, I turn on my fireplace and a few lamps in the living room. The flames in our fireplace ignite with the flip of a switch. (I admit, this is not as romantic as building a fire with logs that snap and crackle, so sometimes I play a soothing soundtrack of a crackling fire.) If you don't have a fireplace, set a programmable thermostat to turn on the furnace 20 minutes prior to your morning alarm.

A clean pot filled with water and ready to brew tea or coffee also makes the wee hours of the morning more welcoming. The warmth of a hot mug in my hands and the glow of the flickering flames from a fireplace or candles and soft lamps lit on a dark morning become a cue to pause and make the most of the quiet.

There is so much to be grateful for, even in winter. For warmth, for shelter, for family, for health, for a quiet morning, for grace and comforts. Choose which blessings will help you have a soulful start to each day.

GOOD MORNING RITUALS

Inspire your day, mood, and wellness during winter months with simple morning rituals. These starter ideas can spark your own list of what nourishes you.

+ Take a morning prayer walk.

+ Diffuse or apply essential oils that promote a sense of calm.

+ Play a relaxing nature soundtrack to help you drown out other noise or racing thoughts—ocean waves, crackling fires, babbling books, rain.

+ Use a gratitude journal to focus.

+ Write out prayers and read meditations.

+ Study the Bible or a devotional that encourages or challenges you.

+ Stretch and feel grateful for your body.

Be joyful in hope, patient in affliction, faithful in prayer.

ROMANS 12:12

DIFFUSE ESSENTIAL OILS TO INFUSE YOUR SPIRIT

Need a mood boost? Scents are a powerful way to impact the mood of our homes as well as elevate our well-being. They can stir up emotions such as joy and peace as well as remind us of special memories associated with them.

Mix and match your favorite pure essential oils to accompany your daily routines and rituals. They can help you create an uplifting or even meditative mood. Here are some inspiring blends for your diffuser this season.

TRY ANY OF THESE REFRESHING UPLIFTING COMBINATIONS:

CINNAMON BARK + **CLOVE** + **ORANGE**

PEPPERMINT + **VANILLA**

NEROLI + **ORANGE**

VANILLA + **SANDALWOOD**

BERGAMOT + **LIME**

DELIGHT IN TEA AND COFFEE

Yummy, hot beverages warm up your hands and make you feel cozier inside too. I've long been a believer in elevating the morning coffee experience so it is more than just a rushed jolt of caffeine from a paper cup on the mad dash to work.

I'm not claiming to be a barista, but as a Seattleite and Pacific Northwesterner for many years, I admit I've become a bit of an accidental coffee snob. It took some experimentation to develop the perfect cup, but now I love our homemade coffee as much or more as any six-dollar-plus cup of coffee I've tried.

Make it a slow and savored experience. It can be a morning ritual that you will look forward to in every way.

Set up a simple winter beverage station with everything you need. Gather your favorite mugs and have them ready! You can even let guests choose their own mug if you have friends or family who want to join you.

My favorite morning beverage starts with freshly ground organic coffee beans (I love beans with a hint of chocolate) and steamed oat milk. Occasionally we add vanilla, cocoa, maple syrup, or even a pinch of sea salt to jazz it up!

Some afternoons or evenings we make tea. My favorites are chai, Earl Grey, blueberry chamomile, and lavender tea. Tea is a special ritual all its own (I like to visualize the tea ceremony at the Empress Hotel in Victoria; it's quite an experience).

Years ago, I started sharing my morning coffee ritual with my friends online by creating a short daily video. I recorded the sound of my beans grinding and the coffee bubbling from the percolator on our gas stove. Everyone loved watching the steam rising from the mug as the coffee was poured. Finally, I added the rich, thick foam of the steamed oat milk on top and finished with a swirl of cinnamon.

While I couldn't hand a cup of coffee to anyone watching through the screen, nor could I share a scratch and sniff of the comforting aroma that wafted through the kitchen, I was blown away by hundreds of people commenting on how relaxing it was to watch. It inspired many to start their own at-home coffee or tea ritual.

It's the little things that make a ritual more meaningful. Even if you don't have time to savor your coffee every morning, make it a special experience as often as you can.

Give your coffee a cozy winter flavor with a bit of...

PEPPERMINT	MAPLE
NUTMEG	HAZELNUT
CLOVE	CARAMEL
CARDAMOM	BROWN SUGAR
COCOA	CINNAMON SUGAR
VANILLA	

Top with whipped cream (or coconut cream).

He made the moon to mark the seasons, and the sun knows when to go down.

PSALM 104:19

HOMEMADE OATMEAL

What better way to accompany your morning coffee than with a hot steaming bowl of oatmeal? It is a comforting way to start the day. Whether you slow cook your oats or make instant oatmeal, the addition of toppings will take your oatmeal from bland to brilliant:

DATES

DRIED GOJI/WOLFBERRIES

DRIED OR FRESH BERRIES AND FRUIT

CHOPPED NUTS

COCONUT FLAKES

VANILLA

SHAVED CHOCOLATE

MAPLE SYRUP

BROWN SUGAR

HEMP SEEDS

NUT BUTTER

STEAMED AND FOAMED MILK (OR TRY ALMOND OR OAT MILK)

If you have picky eaters at home, create a small topping buffet with different options each week to keep your family interested in a healthy start to their day. And in winter, oatmeal makes a very enjoyable afternoon or evening treat too.

ADD CREATIVITY—THE SPICE OF LIFE

Feeling uninspired in the doldrums of winter? Try a new hobby! There's no better place to explore your creative side than in your own home. Don't worry about how a project or pursuit might turn out; just let yourself relax and enjoy. Invite all your family members to choose a winter hobby this year.

+ Gather a few painting supplies and small canvases or a sketchbook to bring out your inner artist.

+ Join a book or writing group to savor stories and connect with others.

+ Fill a pretty notebook with your thoughts, dreams, and daily stories.

+ Take an online cooking course and try making one meal a week with your family.

Don't expect yourself to do new things perfectly. Give yourself the grace to enjoy the experience and to find pleasure and delight in the process!

He has made everything beautiful in its time. He has also set eternity in the human heart;
yet no one can fathom what God has done from beginning to end.

ECCLESIASTES 3:11

BRING FRIENDS TOGETHER VIRTUALLY

While it's tempting for me (as an Enneagram nine and homebody introvert) to want to stay curled up in the house all winter and avoid most social interaction, I've discovered something surprising—winter is a perfect season to be more intentional in reaching out and nurturing connections. The reconnection that autumn ushered in can continue in gentle ways.

Ideally, relationships are built and maintained face-to-face, yet there are seasons when an online community might be ideal for avoiding isolation or loneliness and embracing new friendships with kindred spirits.

One year, I decided to stop scrolling social media looking for deliverance from the winter doldrums and chose to start scrolling the news feed to connect with friends and bring a bit of encouragement to others.

What a difference this shift made in my own disposition! Sometimes I reached out with a simple, supportive comment. Other times, I posted heartfelt, unsolicited compliments. (You know those nice things that cross your mind as you see someone's photo but you don't always verbalize? Tell them! It will likely make their day.) I sent private messages to friends to let them know I saw what they were going through and was thinking of them. Rather than offering something generic like "I'll be praying for you," I asked them how I could specifically pray for them. Then I put their name on my prayer list so I would follow through.

If you can't get together with others in person, planning a virtual gathering can lift everyone's spirits! We've attended church, hosted Bible studies, invited friends to fun workshops, and hosted family game nights and dinner parties, all virtually. It's never quite as warm and wonderful as being face-to-face or hugging people in person, but it's the next best thing to being there.

Winter can be an isolating time for many. What could you do in this season to bring friends together?

TABLE GAMES AND TRADITIONS

We can slow down a hectic rhythm of long days filled to the brim with frantic activity and make room in winter for a more soulful, joyful life. Many traditions become touchstones that cue our bodies, minds, and spirits to release burdens and lean into familiar, restful practices.

My mom always has the best ideas for making a house a home. Growing up, we had game tables. Just as a dining table draws people together for nourishment and conversation, a game table or any dedicated place to enjoy puzzles, board games, and cards draws people together for laughter, joy, and connection.

When my parents had a beach house on the Oregon coast, there was a chess set on a game table right by a big window overlooking the ocean. It was ready to be played on a stormy day or whenever the inspiration struck.

Years ago, my mom gave us one of her beautiful tables (complete with a checker/ chess board stained on the wood top). Our kids played games and did puzzles on that table growing up. My husband still loves to do puzzles on that very table, which currently resides in our living room. Sometimes we even put together a puzzle for date night. We pick puzzles with scenes to reflect the season we're in—snowy land-scapes in the winter, boats and villages by the sea in the summer—and in every season, I love images of charming homes.

MAKE SEASONAL MEMORIES

The best winter holiday traditions bring people together and leave a lasting impression. Keep them simple and sustainable, and give yourself permission to let go or evolve to new traditions.

Some choices will have spiritual meaning. My friend Darlene's family waits until Christmas morning to add Baby Jesus to their nativity scene. Some traditions will be about regularly celebrating a family member or memory. Here are a few ideas. Which ones might serve you and your family this year?

+ Make a gratitude tree. Write down what you are grateful for on leaf-shaped paper.

+ Host an annual pie or chili bake-off (with prizes).

+ Have a Christmas hideous-sweater party.

+ Start soup and game nights.

+ Attend a candlelight Christmas Eve service.

+ Go Christmas caroling.

+ Get new jammies and have a family slumber party.

+ Host a cookie exchange party.

+ Choose a new ornament each year to represent a memory or family member.

+ Make gingerbread houses.

+ Begin a favorite holiday-movie night.

+ Pack gifts for or volunteer for families in need.

+ Tour neighborhood lights.

+ Have a fondue night.

+ Give gifts in four categories: want, need, wear, read.

+ Use advent calendars.

+ Draw names for friend or family gift-giving.

+ Host a video chat with extended family.

+ Dress up on Christmas Eve regardless of whether you have somewhere to go.

+ Take a family photo every Christmas; use the same theme each year.

TWO WAYS TO GIVE FROM THE HEART

Make the holiday personal and meaningful. It doesn't take much effort to sprinkle in delight and connection. This is how memories and traditions are made.

1. *Give creative experiences.* Experiences make us happier and more creative, and they bring people together. Instead of wrapping up yet another thing to clutter your life, create a special package representing the gift of a meaningful experience.

MUSIC LESSONS	**PUZZLE NIGHT**
GAME NIGHT	**POTTERY PAINTING**
SCAVENGER HUNT	**MAKE-YOUR-OWN PIZZA NIGHT**
PAINTING KIT	**COOKING CLASSES**
KNITTING LESSONS	**PARTY IN A BOX**
CAMPING SUPPLIES	**INDOOR PICNIC**
FAMILY DANCE LESSONS	**CRAFT NIGHT**

2. *Wrap gifts in personal, seasonal ways.* Look around your home, craft closet, and yard for special touches to make your packages personal and reflective of the season.

+ Use brown or white craft paper with a fun patterned ribbon.

+ Make your own gift tags from printed family photos.

+ Add a touch of nature with sprigs of pine or eucalyptus.

+ Make your own gift wrap personalized with permanent markers or rubber stamps.

+ Tie on fun embellishments such as bells, ornaments, monograms, or small added gifts.

GOOD NIGHT RITUALS

Set yourself up for a restful night with these habits and rituals. This self-care will not only prepare you for needed sleep but also infuse your days with more energy and joy. Ensure a restful evening by choosing consistent timing for going to bed and awakening.

+ Clear away clutter so your space is calm and inviting.

+ Make a list of things to deal with tomorrow so you can clear your mind.

+ Brew and sip a cup of herbal tea.

+ Write down three things you're grateful for.

+ Spray your sheets with a lavender linen spray.

+ Turn off electronic gadgets earlier in the evening to let your mind know it's time to wind down.

+ Do a puzzle, read a relaxing book, or get in a warm bath (add candlelight, essential oils, and soft music for the ultimate hygge experience).

+ Use a glow serum on your face before bed.

+ Turn off bright lights and use the softer glow of fairy lights or twinkling trees.

RESTORATIVE HOME SPA TREATMENTS

No need to shop the aisles or online storefronts for serums and scrubs. These are easy DIY recipes to inspire beauty and restoration. Create one or all four, and make enough to share with a friend or two. This is a season to pamper your body and soul.

Relaxing Evening Glow Serum

+ 10 drops frankincense

+ 10 drops copaiba

+ 10 drops melaleuca

+ 5 drops lavender

+ 5 drops geranium

+ 5 drops cypress

+ 2 drops blue tansy

Fill a roller bottle with oils and top with jojoba oil or any carrier oil of your choice. Swirl to blend.

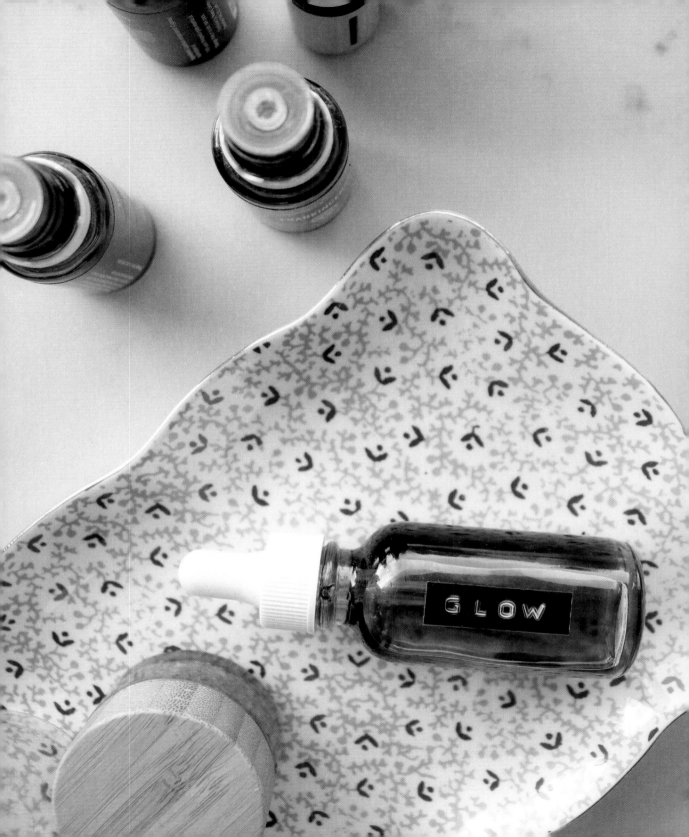

Winter Night Lip Scrub

+ 2 tsp. brown sugar

+ 1 tsp. coconut oil

+ 1 squeeze of honey

+ 2 drops peppermint oil

Apply to lips and wipe clean for exfoliation.

Relaxing Massage Oil

Warm ½ cup of sweet almond oil with 20 drops of any relaxing essential oil (lavender, chamomile, cedarwood, bergamot). Soothe onto sore muscles or dry skin areas for a wonderful wintertime home spa session.

Soothing Oatmeal Bath

+ 2 cups finely ground organic oatmeal (grind in a blender)

+ 2 cups organic Epsom salts

+ 20 drops essential oils of your choice (lavender would be lovely!)

Add to a warm bath.

DREAM OF SPRING

If winter starts to feel dreary, it helps to remind ourselves that spring is on the way. Keep a pretty notebook where you can jot down all the lovely ideas that pop into your head during the day (or in the wee hours of the night). Whether the possibilities are destined for next season or next year, it is inspiring to keep track of what you love!

I have a folder on my phone where I collect ideas I see on social media and online. I love to dream and plan, and keeping my ideas organized for a future season makes the winter more enjoyable.

"For I know the plans I have for you," declares the Lord, *"plans to prosper you and not to harm you, plans to give you hope and a future."*

JEREMIAH 29:11

WINTER LOVE LETTERS

+ Write a letter to someone you admire to thank them for the impact they've had on you.

+ Buy a few cups of coffee and take them to your neighbors.

+ Pack up gently used or new items to share with others.

+ Give more hugs.

+ Plan a family "restaurant night in." Let the kids make menus. Decorate the space like you were at a restaurant table with candles and cozy lighting.

◇

The best and most beautiful things in the world cannot be seen or even touched—they must be felt with the heart.

HELEN KELLER

LINGER ON LOVELINESS

We all have *unlovely* moments. They happen. The unfortunate times when the dog barfs on the carpet. (Why, oh why can't they choose an easier surface to clean?) When the dishwasher overflows—invariably right before guests are about to arrive. The days when we're frustrated, deadlines are stressing us out, our heads are pounding, and our homes are out of control. There are seasons of life where we will grieve and many situations that make it difficult to keep a smile on our faces. Yet as my mother-in-law would remind us in any trying situation, "This too shall pass." And it will.

A lovely life is shaped through the ebb and flow of all seasons, molded by the moments we choose to savor. We can't expect season after season of ideal days all strung together, at least this side of heaven. But on many days, we can put one foot in front of the other in the direction we want to go. One routine task can be made a bit more lovely. One small moment of joy can be treasured in our hearts. We can discover our own rituals that inspire and prepare us to grow and bloom with gratitude. We can find a rhythm to inhale *and* exhale. Connect *and* disconnect. Refresh *and* retreat.

There really is a season for everything under the sun. Everything can be made more beautiful in time. Make room in your day to linger on the loveliness in front of you at this moment, whatever it may be. These moments will bring peace and comfort to your soul, joy and beauty to your surroundings, and more grace to the world.

I hope you keep this book close to you, like a friend, to encourage you as you bring loveliness to your home, life, and community in every season.

ACKNOWLEDGMENTS

In the summer of 2007 I sat at my bedroom desk staring at a computer screen. I had just started my decorating business, The Inspired Room, earlier that same year and was enjoying helping others make their homes feel more pulled together and to reflect their own style using things they already had. The Inspired Room was an answer to prayer in that season, but little did I know, it was only the beginning of what was to come.

My friend Shelley's husband, Rick, had suggested on several occasions that I start a blog. And what exactly would I use a blog for, I asked? It seemed like one more thing I probably didn't have time for. I really didn't know much about the world of blogging and I certainly didn't know it was going to change our lives in so many incredible ways! Eventually I decided it sounded like it could be a good way to connect with more people and on a whim one day, without a plan, I decided I would give a blog a try.

So I typed the words "hello, world" and introduced myself to my computer screen. And just like that, a delightful new adventure began.

One by one, I discovered there are other house-shaped heart people in the world. Kindred spirits who also find joy in the simple pleasures of home in every season. I found my people and began blogging full time.

As the years went by, my daughters Kylee and Courtney grew into young women who became creators of their own homes. They joined me in the vision for The Inspired Room. Our book agents Ruth, Bill, and Teresa and publishing team at Harvest House saw the heart behind what we did and together (along with the support of my husband Jerry and son Luke) we began creating a lovely series of books.

It still feels surreal to me that the answer to so many of our family's prayers through the years has been to continue to share a passion for the home. My parents demonstrated a love of creating a home as I was growing up and I'm so grateful that I have been able to use that gift as a foundation for my own simple offering. It has carried us all through many difficult days, made so many dreams come true and has brought a lot of joy to our lives to share it with others.

We feel blessed to be able to do what we love while being surrounded by a wonderful community of like-minded friends. We are so grateful.

(Special thanks to my friend Susan Heid of *The Confident Mom* for allowing me to include the photos I took at her lovely beach home in Seabrook, Washington.)

◇

"Friendship is born at that moment when one person says to another,
'What! You too? I thought I was the only one.'"

C.S. LEWIS

OTHER BOOKS
BY MELISSA

Live Your Lovely Life

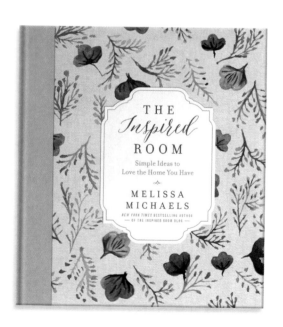

BUT WHERE DO I PUT *the couch?*

&
Answers to 100 Other
Home Decorating Questions

Melissa Michaels
The Inspired Room
KariAnne Wood
Thistlewood Farms

NEW YORK TIMES BESTSELLER

LOVE *the* H🌍ME *you* HAVE

Simple Ways to... Embrace Your Style • Get Organized • Delight in Where You Are

MELISSA MICHAELS
Author of *The Inspired Room* blog

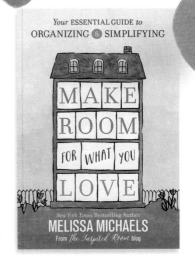

Your ESSENTIAL GUIDE *to*
ORGANIZING & SIMPLIFYING

MAKE ROOM FOR WHAT YOU LOVE

New York Times Bestselling Author
MELISSA MICHAELS
FROM *The Inspired Room* blog

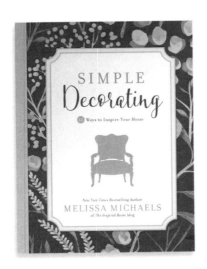

SIMPLE *Decorating*

50 Ways to Inspire Your Home

New York Times Bestselling Author
MELISSA MICHAELS
of The Inspired Room blog

SIMPLE *Gatherings*

50 Ways to Inspire Connection

New York Times Bestselling Author
MELISSA MICHAELS
of The Inspired Room blog

SIMPLE *Organizing*

50 Ways to Clear the Clutter

New York Times Bestselling Author
MELISSA MICHAELS
of The Inspired Room blog

ABOUT THE
AUTHOR

Melissa Michaels is the creator of *The Inspired Room* (theinspiredroom.net) and twice voted *Better Homes & Gardens* Reader's Favorite Decorating Blogger. Her mission is to inspire women to create homes they can't wait to come home to.

She is also the author of several popular home decorating and lifestyle books, including the *New York Times* bestseller *Love the Home You Have, Dwelling, Simple Decorating*, and *The Inspired Room* coffee table book.

Melissa has a passion for helping readers find contentment at home, encouraging them to embrace each season, experience peace and comfort in rhythms and routines, to welcome others into their home, and care for their well-being by keeping their lives and homes clean and simple. In 2015, Melissa and her daughters launched Dwell Well Collective, a wellness community for women who are investing in their homes, bodies, minds, and lives.

Melissa and her husband recently became empty nesters for the first time and live in their new dream home near the beautiful San Juan Islands in Washington state.